An old adage says, "Those who can, do, and those who can't, teach." Bishop David Evans blows this saying away, inasmuch as he is a teacher who also "does." His ministry at Bethany Baptist Church is wide-reaching in its scope. This gifted communicator seems to have a passion for bringing to wholeness anyone who is hurting. In an age of pop psychology and easy answers, he dares to believe that emotional scars are not necessary if we serve the same God the Bible reveals to us—the God we see active in the lives of both Old and New Testament saints.

David Evans is a skilled soul-physician, and in his hands, many lives have been incredibly metamorphosed from tremendous pain to awesome delight. The message of the "three Hebrew boys" is still the same: If God can do it for them, He can do it for anyone. This message is desperately needed in an age when Christians are being encouraged to "live with it" or "get over it." David Evans' message is sorely needed in the church today.

Joseph L. Garlington, Sr., Ph.D.
Senior Pastor, Covenant Church of Pittsburgh
Presiding Bishop, Reconciliation Ministries International!

Bishop David Evans comes to the body of Christ with a book that is based on his vast experience, which includes the tremendous suffering and persecution he has had to endure. Ministry on any level demands sacrifice (a price must be paid), and he has paid the price. So then, this book will release healing, anointing, and blessing.

Bishop Tudor Bismark
Jabula-New Life Ministries International

Bishop Evans is an insightful instructor of spiritual truth. I know that the anointed revelation God has given him will assist you in getting to your next level.

Pastor Chip Radke
God's House Westbank Cathedral
New Orleans, Louisiana

Healed Without
SCARS

Healed Without SCARS

DAVID G. EVANS

WHITAKER
HOUSE

HEALED WITHOUT SCARS

David G. Evans
1115 Gibbsboro Road
Lindenwold, NJ 08021
e-mail: d.evans1@rcn.com
website: www.abundantharvest.com

ISBN-13: 978-0-88368-542-6
ISBN-10: 0-88368-542-6
Printed in the United States of America
© 2004 by David G. Evans

1030 Hunt Valley Circle
New Kensington, PA 15068
website: www.whitakerhouse.com

Library of Congress Cataloging-in-Publication Data

Evans, David G. (David Gregory)
Healed without scars / David G. Evans.
p. cm.
ISBN 0-88368-542-6 (trade pbk. : alk. paper)
1. Spiritual healing. 2. Healing—Religious aspects—Christianity. I. Title.
BT732.5.E83 2004
248.8'6—dc22
2004010006

---

4 5 6 7 8 9 10 11 12 13 14 15 **ω** 14 13 12 11 10 09 08 07 06 05

Dedication

In memory of my grandfather, Albert Quincy Prince—God's gift of wisdom, patience, dedication, productive manhood, consistency, and love.

Acknowledgments

I want to thank Bob Whitaker, Jr., for taking an interest in an unknown author during a season of transition.

To John David Kudrick, who told me to "show them, not tell them." Thank you for your guidance and wisdom.

To Lois Puglisi, the translator of my thoughts. Thanks for perceiving my sensitivity and encouraging me to stick to my inspiration.

To Yolanda and Lisa, for overruling my complacency and making contact with Whitaker House on my behalf.

To the rest of the *Healed Without Scars* book staff, Val and Chrystal, for always figuring out what to do and how to do it. Thanks.

To all those who will be helped by this book.

Thanks to my family, my Bethany family, those close to my heart, for praying for and believing in me.

And most of all, to God, for the inspiration and thematic revelation He gives.

Contents

Foreword

The capacity to lead is marked clearly by the capacity to serve. The choice that a leader makes about serving determines the level of success, accomplishment, wholeness, well-being, and potential of those being led. In an era when dysfunction has become an acceptable buzzword and individuals find themselves continually sorting through unfinished business from their pasts, it takes a courageous and cutting-edge individual to embrace and evoke the possibility of a radically new world, a world where you can be healed without the residue of scars from the past.

A prophetic leader lives out of a creative paradigm, which casts a vision of healing for individuals that is based on where they are going and not where they have been. Such leaders invite those whom they lead into a world they deeply want to belong to, yet rarely ever experience until that leader creates a path for them to get there. The book you are holding was written by such a leader—a servant-leader!

The kind of world that he leads you to is one where people are healed to such a degree that there are no scars remaining within or without. The message of that truth is waiting for all who dare to believe it exists and are prepared to embrace a powerful vision of their future in God.

Bishop David Evans is a compelling leader with a compelling vision because he has been gripped by a compelling future. You hold in your hands not simply a book, but also a life experience. This experience will open the pathway to being elegantly healed without scars by the One who bore the scars on your behalf. You can't be around the likes of a servant-leader like Bishop Evans without experiencing the irresistible healing presence of Christ inviting you into a world that you have always wanted to belong to, yet never knew how to access.

Bishop Evans' insights on the healing process and the power of God to do the seemingly impossible will present some difficulties for those who are looking for a reason to stay in their unfinished business and wear their former pains as badges of survival. His insights about the nature of the life that is healed without scars, available to everyone who dares to believe, will become a chariot of fire to catch you up into realms of transcendent glory.

Healed Without Scars takes you on a journey of healing, wholeness, well-being, possibility, and prophetic potential. Bishop Evans leaves no room for anything less than total recovery and restoration. In the process, he connects with the part of all of us that wrestles with the profound changes required in today's dysfunctional world to rise above it all. If that weren't enough, he then gives us the wings to do so.

When you grasp what the Spirit of God is endeavoring to tell you through the message in this book, it will be totally impossible for you to walk away from it with the idea that your scars must be with you forever. In addition, it will be impossible for your life to ever be the same again!

Dr. Mark J. Chironna
Overseer, The Master's Touch International Church
Orlando, Florida

"O God the Lord, for thy name's sake: because thy mercy is good, deliver thou me. For I am poor and needy, and my heart is wounded within me."

—Psalm 109:21–22

Introduction:
Life's Fiery Furnaces

Three men found themselves in a very uncomfortable place—a fiery furnace. It was a situation that should have ended their existence, but somehow they survived. At the very least the experience should have left them emotionally and physically scarred. The evidence of this experience should have been obvious to everyone around them, yet it wasn't. Why?

Shadrach, Meshach, and Abednego survived because God was literally in the midst of their experience. Because of this vital factor, they emerged from the furnace with their identities, self-esteem, and emotions apparently unaffected, with no evidence of this negative past upon them.

The Secret of the Presence

How have you fared in life's "fiery furnaces"? Most of us allow the fires of life to burn and scar us. This is because we don't yet know the secret of living in the presence of God even in the midst of our difficulties and trials.

The trauma of negative experiences—broken homes, child abuse, fractured relationships, squandered opportunities, and unfulfilled expectations—has a profound effect on all of us. While we are often wounded in our early years, the aftermath of our experiences persists throughout our lives. We somehow hope that time alone will heal the pain of the past, only to discover that the old adage, "Time heals all wounds," is woefully incorrect. Time does heal some of our wounds. But time alone is powerless to heal all of them. It also cannot remove the layers of scars that build up on our emotions when our pain is unresolved. Rather than being healed, our wounds actually grow larger—producing relational, social, and spiritual difficulties.

One of the great dilemmas many people face today is trying to function productively while bearing the injuries that life inflicts. Often, in order to survive, we retreat into a safe place within ourselves that helps to shield our emotions but, at the same time, stunts our emotional growth. We struggle day to day, hiding behind masks of success, confidence, education, or political correctness. Privately struggling with issues of the past, we fight a losing battle within the isolation of our thoughts and emotions. We appear to mature while, in reality, we struggle inwardly to develop as men and women. When we are adults, facing adult challenges and expectations, our immaturity and unresolved issues sabotage vital relationships and opportunities.

Yet trauma does much more than rob us of portions of our lives. It seeks to consume our very identities and robs us of our peace. We appear to live "normal" lives—going to work, raising families, and making plans for the future—while secretly dealing with the shock of unresolved hurt. The distress of these situations often causes us to feel confused and betrayed. Trauma isolates, alienates, and leaves us feeling as though the future holds nothing positive for us.

Though all of us have come through fiery situations in life, we have experienced a variety of effects from them. Some of us exhibit no visible evidence of injury, while others bear obvious emotional scars. Sometimes, we're not aware of the effects of the fire until well after the incident, when a wound or scar suddenly seems to manifest itself. When this happens, we are often bewildered at the intensity of the pain.

Again, the answer to our hurt is in learning to live in God's presence. Many people are surprised to discover that they can love God and be reconciled to Him through faith in Christ, yet still continue to be deeply wounded and heavily scarred from the fires of abuse, rejection, depression, abandonment, disappointment, and hopelessness. When they hear that God can deliver them, they passionately "proclaim" their healing—while continuing to suffer. In this way, they are often contradictory fountains, producing both sweet and bitter water at the same time.

Living in Wholeness

We need to understand how to allow God to heal our wounds and scars so that we can be whole people. Your heavenly Father wants you to know that (1) He has the power to heal you of your past wounds and scars, and (2) in the future fires of life, He can—as He did for Shadrach, Meshach, and Abednego—deliver you from being scarred by tragic experiences so that they won't have any lasting negative effects on you.

Let God come into the fire of your experiences. His love and compassion will transform your anger, sense of injustice, loss of identity, and alienation as you emerge unscarred from the fires of your life. As you read this book, you will find the courage to open the dusty box of your past. *Healed Without Scars* provides you with a safe haven in the privacy of your own thoughts to acknowledge your wounds and scars and to allow Jesus to heal you.

You may find yourself in these pages; or you may recognize loved ones and friends and finally discover a way to assist them in overcoming the emotional weights in their lives. This book is written to the multitudes who, like me, have endured the pains, disappointments, and shame of the past. It is a ladder that will assist them step-by-step in their climb out of life's valley, which is shadowed by negative events and experiences. Though it is written with the Christian community in mind, it is relevant to all who have wondered, "Will I ever feel any differently? Will the pain ever go away?"

Grace, like rain, falls on the "just and the unjust," the saved and the unsaved. Through this book, God will lead you to a healing that is evident to you and also obvious to others. The fire of your experiences has no power over the present. The heat of past challenges is unable to permanently alter the positive maturation of your personality. You can have the security of coming through the ups and downs of life with your sense of self intact. God will give you the gift of a new life that will clear away the burnt aroma of victimization that continually sabotages the meaningful events and relationships of your life. As you receive your heavenly Father's touch, you will be *Healed Without Scars*.

Chapter One

The Wounds and Scars of Life

Is pain from your past holding you back?

I was settled into my seat on the airplane, but it didn't look as if we were going anywhere soon. The plane was waiting on the runway for permission to take off from Dallas International Airport. All around me, I could hear the usual protests from those who thought our plane should just nudge the others out of the way and take off. Tension born of impatience and inconvenience began to fill the cabin. As if he could sense the passengers' mood, a child two rows behind me started crying. Nearby, a woman talked loudly into her cell phone. She was attempting to give all who were in earshot the impression that she had some influence with the airline—but she was traveling in coach with the rest of us.

Slowly, I realized that it was getting hot in the cabin. Warm air was hissing from the overhead vents. I could feel the tension rise even more with the increased temperature. Someone a number of rows away coughed—guaranteeing that the passengers would share his germs as well as the flight. The shoulder-bruising service cart began to make its way up the aisle. Then the lights went out in the cabin. It was now dusk both inside the airplane and out, except for overhead lights above some of the passengers' seats.

We continued to wait our turn. I began to wonder if there was a spiritual purpose for the delayed flight. It was one of those situations in which conversation with your seatmate becomes almost mandatory. I didn't really feel like talking to anyone, so I was trying to hide in plain sight by reading my Bible. I have found that reading the Word can polarize people into those who want to avoid you and those who are truly looking for life's answers.

A Mixture of Disappointment and Hope

The woman sitting next to me began to move around in her seat, breaking my concentration. I wondered whether she was nervous about air travel. Once again, I promised myself that I would fly first class in the future. When I looked up in response to one of her movements, she quickly seized the opportunity and started a conversation with me. The pilot came on the intercom saying that we had been cleared for takeoff. As we taxied down the runway, Del began to talk to me about her life. Apparently, it wasn't fear of flight that was making her restless; it was something deeper. I closed my Bible and began to listen. I knew at once that the Holy Spirit was involved in our meeting.

Del's tone was one that I had heard many times before. It was a mixture of disappointment and guarded hope. It was obvious that she had told her story to many other people, looking for some sense, some explanation for her broken life.

She began by unfolding her story tentatively, one layer at a time. Then her words began to overflow, not because I was listening, but because she could see that I understood. She spoke of her childhood tragedies, her history of broken relationships and lost opportunities, and her despair for the future. I realized that for her, as with many other people, the scar-producing pain of her past had become the blueprint for her present and the structure of her vision for her future.

When Del was a child, her parents had given her up for adoption. Over the years, she had developed a shell of protection. You could feel her defensiveness. She had experienced the ultimate rejection—greater than the rejection of an employer, friend, or boyfriend: Neither parent wanted her.

> The pain of her past had become the blueprint for her present and the vision for her future.

She had been in so many foster homes that eventually she had forced herself to lose count. In the process, she had experienced various levels of treatment from those she was living with—from brutal to loving, abusive to caring. In order to survive, she had developed her own protective world. This world did not allow reality to factor into her life. When things became too difficult, she simply retreated into her shell. She no longer felt that she could really trust anyone.

As Del talked, I began to recognize another tone in her voice that was not evident at first. I was looking at a woman, but I was talking to a child. Her appearance had deceived me. Hidden inside an adult facade was a child pleading for rescue. Occasionally, the injured child in her would reveal herself with an immature response to a question or a pouting expression when an inconsistency in her story was pointed out.

The most revealing part of the conversation was that she had been a Christian for about fifteen years. Some of her wounds had been inflicted before she was saved and some after her conversion, but the resulting scars were very evident. Becoming a Christian, in itself, hadn't alleviated the pain from her wounded past.

The Holy Spirit shifted my approach in talking with her. I realized that, while her adult mind had an objective acceptance of the reality of God, the child in her did not trust her personal relationship with Him. She feared that God would give her away just as everyone else had. The child within her was pleading for love while the woman she had become was searching for acceptance. Her problem was evident to me: She was struggling with shame because she had been trying to satisfy the need of the child in so-called adult ways.

Although genuinely caring people had come into her life, her fear had caused her to reject both male and female friends. She attempted intimacy with many, trying to satisfy the ache of both the child and the adult. She placed herself in one compromising sexual situation after another, never saying no to anyone or anything. Those she was intimate with, she eventually pushed away. Those who had no sexual interest in her, she found a reason to distrust.

Del despised who she had become. She'd been wounded by others, and she had wounded herself. As a result, she could not hold down a job, maintain her finances, or develop true friendships. Anger always simmered beneath the surface of her life.

I have learned that nothing seems to scar as deeply as an emotional wound. Since I know the truth of that reality from personal experience, I assured Del that she was not alone in her pain. I began sharing with her some of my own defeats and victories in life, in both childhood and adulthood. I didn't tell her these things for the purpose of relieving her hurt, but in order to give her a frame of reference for her pain. From my own life, as well as my experience in counseling others, I have learned that company in misery is no real consolation. Just knowing that others have suffered doesn't necessarily relieve our own suffering. It is deliverance from misery that brings consolation, hope, and healing, and that was what Del really needed.

> Nothing seems to scar as deeply as an emotional wound.

The Father's Touch

The words *father* and *mother* come with a long list of expectations, and when these expectations aren't met, the emotional consequences can be great. In Del's life, the situation was especially complex. I knew that I first had to reach the adult in order to position the child for healing. I explained to her that her parents had both strengths and weaknesses, just like everybody else. One of their weaknesses was that they had lacked the tools to effectively parent her.

I told her that I didn't think her father and mother had given her away out of hatred, but because they felt that they were not equipped for the job of parenting. They knew that they were missing something inside. They had put her up for adoption with the hope that someone else would do what they could not do. Her being given away was *not her fault*.

The woman heard me, and the child began to cry. She said, "I thought something was wrong with me." I reminded her that, despite the foster homes, the lifestyle choices, the broken relationships, the shame, pain, and guilt, she had survived. Even though there had been times when the voice of Satan had told her to kill herself, she was still alive. I told her that she had not been allowed to die because God had His hand on her and was still working out His purposes in her life. The enemy must have been aware of God's purposes for her because he had tried very hard to destroy her. But the Lord was with her; He had not abandoned her.

The heavenly Father had looked into the nursery of the rejected and had chosen her, saying, "I want *that* one." I shared Romans 8:15 with her: *"For ye have not received the spirit of bondage again to fear; but ye have received the Spirit of **adoption**, whereby we cry, Abba, Father"* (emphasis added).

> Our heavenly Father promises never to leave or forsake us.

On the day that she was saved, she had not received a spirit of bondage. She had received the Spirit of adoption with the power to overcome her fear of the future. Now she could cry *"Abba"* or "Daddy." She could call God her Father.

As I told her this, the power of the Word of God was working to transform her outlook. Del realized that God had always been there with her, and she began to look to Him to answer the child's cry for love and the adult's plea for relationship. But something was still unresolved within her. She asked me one last question: "Considering all the things that I have done, does God still love me?" After all the years that she'd been saved, she was still testing God's love. I told her that God would never leave her or forsake her. (See Hebrews 13:5.) She wept. The hard shell that had formed from years of scarring was broken, and she finally began to heal. She had experienced the Father's touch.

Years later, Del called me after seeing my ministry on television. She told me that she was successfully married, had her own children now, and was working in ministry and helping others with histories similar to hers. The flight from Dallas had been her defining moment. Until that time, her life had been stalled from moving forward. The hurts of her past had been blocking her heart and restricting her freedom.

Like many other people, Del had missed opportunities for deliverance because she had misunderstood God's love, acceptance, and power to heal. Once she understood these things, however, her scars were removed, and her wounds were finally healed.

What Scars Are You Bearing?

To varying degrees, we all suffer from the pains of emotional and psychological wounds, and we bear the hard scars that are the aftermath of these experiences. What pains of disappointment, regret, fear, or abuse are holding you back in life? Whether from broken homes, abusive relationships, disconnection from loved ones through death or abandonment, or lost opportunities, our wounds have torn away our peace and separated us from our strength and vitality.

To be healed, we first have to realize that being hurt is an inescapable part of life in the fallen world we live in. The problem comes when the pain of our past controls the way we live our lives today and shatters our faith and hope for a positive future.

As it did for Del, perhaps the scar-producing pain of your past has become the blueprint for your present. It hinders your relationships, your job, your dreams for your life, and your ability to fulfill those dreams. You've built a protective wall around yourself, which is really a prison that provides no escape from your frustration and despair.

If you are a Christian, you may be feeling guilty or bewildered because there doesn't seem to be any consistency to your life of faith. You're on a roller coaster ride: One day you're up—full of faith and love—and the next day you're down—ready to throw in the towel. You feel you should be living in victory, but all you seem to experience is defeat.

What hurts are holding you back in life?

The Infinite Realm of Possibility

If you struggle with any type of unresolved hurt, I want to invite you into what I call the infinite realm of possibility in God. Your heavenly Father wants to give you a new blueprint for your life—one of His design—that will move you beyond the pain and scars into a meaningful and fulfilling existence. In this realm of possibility, you will understand what it means to live in the presence of your heavenly Father. In His presence, you will find rest from your hurts and a renewed vision for your future. God loves you and will never abandon you in your pain and loneliness. He will bind up your wounds and gently remove your scars so that you can be whole, at peace with yourself and others, and living in the fullness that He created you to live in. Come, let's enter together into that realm of possibility....

Chapter Two

Created to Be Whole

— ◆ —

God's intent for your life is wholeness,
fruitfulness, and increase.

A ll of us have experienced having our hearts wounded.
We brought some of the hurt on ourselves, while other
hurts were forced upon us. Because we are unable to
fix our own emotional pain, most of us have learned to just
cope with it. We are the walking wounded, externally fulfilling our responsibilities while bleeding internally from unresolved issues. While we may participate in this drama called
life, we answer every curtain call with less than our best per-
formance.

This kind of existence is just a shadow of the life that God
desires for you. You may feel as though time and opportunity
have been lost forever as you've been emotionally paralyzed
by hurt and disappointment. Yet God says in His Word that
He is a redeemer of time. He says that He will return to you
the years, the time, that have been consumed by adversity.
(See Joel 2:25.) The time may have been lost to you, but it has
not been lost to God.

Wholeness in God's Image

God has an original intent concerning you. It may be found in His Word and lived out through your relationship with Him. You were created to be *whole*. The account of Creation in the book of Genesis describes God making mankind in His image and likeness. He endowed men and women with authority and placed them as rulers over all that He had created on earth. (See Genesis 1:26–28.) Mankind was to be the reflected image of God in the world, exercising fruitfulness and increase, replenishing what was depleted, and subduing anything that attempted to get out of control.

God's intent was not just for the first man and woman. You, also, were created to reflect His image and to experience wholeness, fruitfulness, and increase in Him. God wants to heal you of your pain and scars and to restore you to His original purpose—demonstrating the same creative power that He used in forming the world.

> You were created to reflect God's image.

Genesis 1:2 says, *"And the earth was without form, and void; and darkness was upon the face of the deep. And the Spirit of God moved upon the face of the waters."* In Hebrew, the words *"without form"* mean "chaos," "confusion," "empty place," "meaninglessness," or "waste place." (See *Strong's*, #H8414; *NASC*, #H8414.) When we are wounded and scarred by people and circumstances, our lives may be described in a similar way.

God took a chaotic and meaningless earth and created an orderly, peaceful world that was overflowing with meaning. The earth orbited systematically around the sun, the ground flourished with vegetation, animals populated the land, and the crown of creation—mankind—was made to rule over everything with creativity and productivity.

God wants to bring order out of the chaos that you have been living in. He will restore you to your dominion authority by enabling you to be fruitful and to subdue the things that attempt to get out of control in your life. Just as the Spirit of God moved upon the face of the waters and brought about the transformation of the earth from confusion to order, it is the work of the Holy Spirit to activate the image of God in each of us, bringing to life all the things that God has prophetically positioned us to accomplish.

The Bible says, *"Now are we the sons of God, and it doth not yet appear what we shall be"* (1 John 3:2). When God was about to create the world, it was basically a mess. It wasn't evident what it would become once God had spoken life to it. In the same way, we can see only a glimpse of what *we* will be after God has restored peace, order, and meaning to our lives.

God's Word tells of His grace toward us. It is a cup of love that overflows at the point of our need. He is the supplier of all that you lack—physically, relationally, and emotionally. *"And God is able to make all grace abound toward you; that ye, always having all sufficiency in all things, may abound to every good work"* (2 Corinthians 9:8). His Word assures you that He is concerned about the prosperity of your soul as well as the rest of your life. (See 3 John 1:2.)

A Need for Deliverance

I remember a time when I was completely brokenhearted. I came from a home in which my father was a substance abuser. All the negative behaviors consistent with this problem were evident in his life. My mother fought to balance

29

this environment with love, but my father's lifestyle led to the breakup of their marriage.

My grandfather, Albert Prince, stepped in as father to my brother and me. Hearing him pray and listening to him read the Word taught me that it was manly to serve God. He was a quiet but influential force in my life, but then he passed away. This wonderful, giving man was gone from my life. Twice, I had lost a father. The hurt from these losses wounded me and left scars on my heart. I retreated from relationships with other males for about ten years. I thought that I didn't trust other men, but I actually feared bonding with them. It seemed to me that every male I became close to left me. I was afraid to form friendships or mentoring relationships with older males. Then I got saved, and my heart began to mend. I entered into a relationship with the Creator that met my need for a father.

> God will often use you to provide to others what you yourself need.

My heavenly Father took over where my grandfather had left off, and I was progressively healed of my fear. However, I discovered that, even though I was healed, I still needed to be fully delivered from the scars of my past. When God began to use me as a father figure to other men, I came to understand a remarkable spiritual truth: God will often use you to provide to others the very thing that you yourself need. In doing so, He heals you of your own personal insufficiency. As I ministered to others, He healed my wounds and removed my scars.

Anointed to Heal the Brokenhearted

God's plan to restore His original intent for mankind begins with our reconciliation to Him through the ministry and sacrifice of Jesus Christ. Jesus was sent to earth by the Father to be a healer and mender of lives. He declared that the Spirit of the Lord was upon Him to heal hearts that have been broken and to repair lives that have been torn by disappointment and grief:

[Jesus said,] *The Spirit of the Lord is upon me, because he hath anointed me to preach the gospel to the poor; he hath sent me to heal the brokenhearted, to preach deliverance to the captives, and recovering of sight to the blind, to set at liberty them that are bruised.*   (Luke 4:18)

Jesus was sent by God to bring a proclamation of healing and freedom to us. A proclamation is a message that is designed to produce a specific response. I was delivered from my wounds and scars because God empowered Jesus to come to earth with a powerful message that freed me from the captivity caused by my brokenness. He will do the same for you.

Jesus is anointed to do what might seem impossible to you right now: set you free from the chains and confining mind-set of your past. He is looking for people who cannot free themselves from the bondage of repetitive failure and the imprisonment of shame. He is saying, "If you will allow Me, I will fix it."

Will you be made whole? If you will look to Jesus, you will lack nothing because He will supply all your needs. Again, Jesus comes not only to take away our scars, but also to restore us to God's original intent. The Bible says that He is anointed to replace the ashes that come from being burned by life with the beauty of a new perception. *"To give unto them beauty for ashes, the oil of joy for mourning, the garment of praise for the spirit of heaviness"* (Isaiah 61:3).

Jesus will replace the mourning that many of us have experienced—and will experience—with joy. A relationship with Jesus produces wholeness because He restores us to fellowship with our Creator—our heavenly Father—bringing us into the presence and power of God Himself, where the process of true deliverance can occur. Through the renewal of the mind, God will replace your depressive heaviness with a new kind of praise. He will restore your will to rebuild your life. By the power of the Holy Spirit, you will be able to begin again.

The Furnace of Negative Experience

In the introduction to this book, I mentioned the story of three young Hebrew men, Shadrach, Meshach, and Abednego, who were thrown into a fiery furnace and who came out of the experience with no negative effects. King Nebuchadnezzar of Babylon had declared an edict that required them to worship him instead of the living God, but they made a commitment to remain true to their faith. The king became furious. Although the young men had been his trusted and valued advisors, his opinion toward them changed dramatically. Anyone who didn't obey the edict was to be cast into a fiery furnace, and they were no exception. In fact, the king was so angry with them that he ordered his servants to heat the furnace *seven times* hotter than usual and to throw the young men into it. (See Daniel 3:1–20.)

The threat of death by fire was designed to transfer their worship from the true God to a false one—who, in effect, represented their spiritual enemy, Satan. The fiery trials that many

> **Jesus will replace your mourning with joy.**

of us have faced and will face in life have a similar purpose. They are designed to either move our worship away from God or destroy us in the process.

As strong men were sent to bind Shadrach, Meshach, and Abednego, the enemy wants to bind us permanently through our troubles and hurts. Satan desires to restrain you and cast you into the furnace—not a physical binding but a binding of the spirit; not a physical furnace but a potentially tragic circumstance. He knows that, once you are bound in the spirit and trapped in the fires of negative experience, you will begin to miss God's complete purpose for your life. His desire is that the entire ordeal would ultimately destroy your faith, kill your hope, and seal off your promise, leaving you wounded and scarred for life.

God Preserves Us Whole and Complete

This was the situation that the young Hebrew men found themselves in: *"Then these men were bound in their coats, their hosen, and their hats, and their other garments, and were cast into the midst of the burning fiery furnace"* (Daniel 3:21). They were thrown into the fire wearing all their clothes. I think that this text can provide a spiritual breakthrough for us in understanding how we can be healed of our wounds and scars. When we are thrown into the fires of negative experience, everything about our lives might be affected, but God can preserve us whole and complete.

Let's consider what the men were wearing when they were thrown into the fire and what this might represent in their—and our—lives. First, they were wearing *"coats."* Coats or outer garments are often the first things you see when meeting a person. A mantle is another word for coat, and when we talk about someone's "mantle," we often refer to that person's identity and life purpose. When we are faced with difficulties, our image or perception of ourselves can be thrown into the fires of adversity and threatened with destruction.

The Bible also says that they were wearing *"hosen."* This word in Hebrew is *pattiysh* or *petash* and is translated as "gown" or "leggings." (See *Strong's,* #H6361; *NASC,* #H6361.) Since these were specifically men's clothes, this garment could represent their gender. The fires of negative experience may also attack our gender identity and our understanding of how God created us.

In addition, the men were wearing what the Bible calls *"other garments,"* which may mean undergarments. I believe that this refers to what is deeply personal or private in our lives. Sometimes, adversity can prevent us from developing intimacy and close relationships with others.

The Bible says that the fiery furnace was so hot that it killed the soldiers who threw the young men into the fire. *"Because the king's commandment was urgent, and the furnace exceeding hot, the flame of the fire slew those men that took up Shadrach, Meshach, and Abednego"* (Daniel 3:22). Notice that the young men were "taken up" and cast into the fire. Negative experiences have a way of creating a season of momentum that takes us closer and closer to destructive situations. Picture the young men's terror in feeling the heat as they approached the furnace and then saw the guards die. I can imagine the battle within their minds and the testing of their faith as they drew closer and closer, only to fall down into the flames.

The sheer terror of such a situation would produce great psychological and emotional disorders in most people. Even though the young men survived, they might have suffered panic, fear, and stress-related disorders. Lifelong trauma was a probability. They should have come out permanently altered—both emotionally and psychologically. It is amazing that they survived physically. Yet I think the greater miracle was their emotional and spiritual wholeness. Let's look at how this situation transpired:

> *Then King Nebuchadnezzar was astonished; and he rose in haste and spoke, saying to his counselors, "Did we not cast three men bound into the midst of the fire?" They answered and said to the king, "True, O king." "Look!" he answered, "**I see four men loose, walking in the midst of the fire; and they are not hurt, and the form of the fourth is like the Son of God.**" Then Nebuchadnezzar went near the mouth of the burning fiery furnace and spoke, saying, "Shadrach, Meshach, and Abed-Nego, servants of the Most High God, come out, and come here." Then Shadrach, Meshach, and Abed-Nego came from the midst of the fire. And the satraps, administrators, governors, and the king's counselors gathered together, and they saw these men **on whose bodies the fire had no power; the hair of their head was not singed nor were their garments affected, and the smell of fire was not on them.** Nebuchadnezzar spoke, saying, "Blessed be the God of Shadrach, Meshach, and Abed-Nego, who sent His Angel and delivered His servants who trusted in Him, and they have frustrated the king's word, and yielded their bodies, that they should not serve nor worship any god except their own God!"* (Daniel 3:24–28 NKJV, emphasis added)

How did the young men survive? It was because Jesus—the Son of God—not only was in the fire with them, but also had accompanied them into the fire. The Lord was with them in every phase of their fiery trial. They had to go into the fire, but they were delivered without experiencing either wounds or scars. Furthermore, their rejection by the king, their binding by the soldiers, and their fiery ordeal had no ill effects on their future.

If we want to be healed and delivered, we have to recognize that God is with us in the fire of our negative experiences and understand that He is *always* present with us. However, we often try a different approach to preservation.

Restored to His Image

Our emotional pains are as real as the physical affliction suffered by the man at the pool of Bethesda. (See John 5:1-9.) We try to deal with our hurt in the same way that he did. He was waiting for a *person* to come and assist him with his healing, and he was waiting for his *circumstances* to change. We often think that the next relationship, the next promotion, or the next opportunity is going to solve our problems. Yet if our answer was in people or opportunities, we would have been healed by now. The man at the pool was surrounded by people, but they all had their own issues to deal with.

> Nothing is beyond God's power to heal or deliver.

It is Jesus who is the answer to our needs. When He was on earth, He went about teaching and preaching the kingdom of God and healing all manner of conditions that people suffered from. (See Matthew 4:23.) There was nothing, no matter what the torment, that was beyond the power of God to heal or deliver.

Jesus has a connection with your pain and is intimately acquainted with your struggles. He is called a *"man of sorrows, and acquainted with grief"* (Isaiah 53:3). His relationship with the pain is not theoretical; it is real. The Bible says that Jesus is a high priest who has been *"touched with the feeling of our infirmities"* (Hebrews 4:15). He understands what it's like to be abandoned, betrayed, discarded, publicly shamed, and hurt by those who should have loved you—because He has experienced these things Himself. He knows what it is like to feel the contempt of others at no fault of His own. He understands the paralyzing power of rejection by those whom He has come to help.

Yet Jesus also knows what it feels like to come through His trials victoriously because He lived in the love and purpose of God. Through Him, you, also, can experience trials and come through them without wounds or scars. It is His desire to call you out of your struggle. Because of His sacrificial death on the cross, your wounds are now His wounds, your pain is His pain, and by His stripes you are healed. (See Isaiah 53:5.)

You can receive God's healing, validating, and confirming touch through Jesus. He is not afraid of the "mess" in your life. You have been prophetically created for wholeness, victory, recovery, and breakthrough. Once you enter into relationship with God, He will breathe life into that which is dying. He will sow a destiny of preservation and fulfillment into the soil of your life. God will spend time with you by His Spirit, speaking to the insufficiencies and hurts in your experience and working to restore your creation in His image. His touch will heal your heart, renew your joy, and make you complete. He will reestablish His original intent for your life—a life of wholeness without scars.

Chapter Three

The Causes of
Our Pain

*Tests, trials, and life's sufferings can leave personal
scars unless we learn to recognize and respond
to them in faith-affirming ways.*

A ccording to *Merriam-Webster's Collegiate Dictionary*, a
scar may be defined as "a lasting moral or emotional
injury." The emotional scars in our lives are painful
reminders that we have suffered hurt in the past and are still
suffering from it. One of the reasons why it's hard to sort
through our pain and find healing is that we don't recognize
that the challenges and difficulties of life come from several different sources—tests, trials, and the fallenness of this
world. These challenges and difficulties can leave personal
scars unless we learn to recognize them for what they are and
respond to them in faith-affirming ways.

Although tests and trials have similar features, they are
distinct. Tests are usually designed to reveal the character or

ability of an individual. The purpose of trials, on the other hand, is to (1) prove what is true and expose what is false in the world and (2) verify God's power, confirm His nature, and validate His reality. In both tests and trials, a person's patience, endurance, or belief may be proved, but the focus is different. Generally, a test reveals the true heart and motives of a person while a trial reveals the true nature and character of God.

Tests of Character

Tests are questions, problems, or physical afflictions designed to determine the knowledge, intelligence, ability, identity, or character of a person. In a biblical test, an individual encounters a situation in which he is coaxed or driven to go in the wrong direction. It is not God who pulls the person in the wrong way. The situation tempts him, and God always provides a choice along with the test. The godly choice is the *"way to escape"* from the temptation. (See 1 Corinthians 10:13.)

> God always provides a choice along with the test.

Life is a series of continuous testing, with each event drawing a response from us while at the same time defining our character. The character and actions of a person are closely connected. In fact, actions often reveal an individual's character.

A Test of Love and Faithfulness

For example, after God placed the first man and woman in the garden of Eden, their love and faithfulness toward their Creator was tested. Let's step back in time and take a look at the nature of their test.

God has made the entire earth, as well as a special place within it, called *Eden*, for mankind to live in. He desires to create beings who will be His reflection in the world. He accomplishes this by molding some dirt from the earth, out of which He forms the first man, Adam.

When God breathes life into Adam, the man awakens to Eden, a place that is already prepared for him. Then God creates Eve to be Adam's wife. Their provision—everything they need—is already supplied to them by God.

At the center of the garden is the Tree of Life, with the Tree of Knowledge of Good and Evil standing nearby. God speaks directly to Adam, saying, "You can eat of all the trees in the garden except for the Tree of Knowledge of Good and Evil." (See Genesis 2:16–17.) Provision is usually accompanied by some restriction. Liberty always includes elements of personal responsibility and constraint so that our freedom will not be abused or exploited.

Mankind's provision (fruit from the trees in the garden) is in close proximity to what is prohibited. The tree that is forbidden to Adam and Eve does not look "evil"—it looks as pleasant to the eyes and as good for food as all the other trees that are permitted them. The nearness of what is forbidden—but attractive—introduces a temptation. This temptation comes through Satan, who deceives Eve and uses her to present it. Adam has to choose between the forbidden and the permitted, between the voice of God and the voice of temptation. Eve is a visible example of disobedience, since she eats the fruit first and then offers it to Adam. Adam has a command from God and an example of disobedience to consider. Choices test character, and Adam's choice would reveal the allegiance of his heart: Would he choose to reflect the nature of God or the nature of Satan?

Up to this time, Adam apparently has been wisely exercising his authority over the dominion that God has given him. He has been living in the image of His Creator by naming the animals and ruling over the garden. His character has reflected his creation in the likeness of God. Yet, now, Adam listens to the voice of temptation and chooses the forbidden. He decides to disobey God, fails the test, and corrupts the character of the entire human race. (See Genesis 3:1–19.)

God has given each person a free will, and we can choose either good or evil. To enable us to grow strong in our faith and to demonstrate our love for Him, God will test us, just as He tested Adam. Choosing what is right **God will test us to enable us to grow in our faith.** can be a painful experience because we sometimes have to give up what we desire for what is higher and better. When we succumb to temptation, as Adam did, we wound ourselves. If we don't learn from our bad choices, ask God's forgiveness, and return to Him, the wounds can become scars that prevent further growth in faith and love, and that block our relationship with Him.

Tests of Trust

Let's look at another example of a biblical test. Further on in Genesis, we read that God tells Abram to embark on a journey. Abram is also given a promise by God that through him all the nations of the world will be blessed. (See, for example, Genesis 12:1–3; 18:18.) Abram and his wife, Sarai, have purpose, direction, and a promise or assurance from God about their future.

They set out on their journey and, at one point, find themselves in a potentially hostile land. They are never really threatened, but Abram devises a plan to deceive the people there because he is afraid for his life. Abram's plan is based on fear, not fact. His reaction to the situation, with the full knowledge of God's will and protection over his life, is proof of a flaw in his character. At the point of choice, he fails the test. (See Genesis 12:10–20.)

Abram and Sarai are tested again as they wait for the son that God has promised them. Impatience (which is usually a product of some level of fear) becomes the catalyst for Sarai to suggest that her servant Hagar take her place as the mother of the promised son. Expediency will often lead to the wrong choice. Abram and Sarai are aware that Hagar is not God's choice to be the mother of the promised child. However, they are afraid that their old age will prevent the fulfillment of God's word. Abram, like Adam, must choose between God's voice and the voice of temptation, between obedience and disobedience. His consent to the plan reveals a flaw in his character. He fails the test by having a son with Hagar. (See Genesis 16:1–4.) His trust and faith in God are not fully developed. However, the biggest test of his life is yet to come.

Abram and Sarai's relationship with God progresses. He affirms His covenant with them and fulfills His promise by enabling Sarai to conceive, giving them the son—Isaac—that they have been longing and waiting for. God also changes their names to Abraham and Sarah. In the Bible, a name change often indicates a change in character.

The fulfillment of a divine covenant is usually connected to the faith or character of the receiver. An incident in Abraham's life shows the extent to which he has grown in these areas. God tests Abraham by commanding him to offer Isaac as a sacrifice. His immediate obedience is an act of faith and righteousness that demonstrates his transformed character. (See Genesis 22:1–18.) God reveals to Abraham that he has passed the test by telling him, *"Lay not thine hand upon the lad, neither do thou any thing unto him: for now I know that thou fearest God, seeing thou hast not withheld thy son, thine only son from me"* (v. 12).

The Trials of Life

A trial is a different set of circumstances from a test. What Shadrach, Meshach, and Abednego experienced in the fiery furnace was a trial, which began when they were asked to take a stand for or against God. Again, the purpose of a trial is to reveal what is genuine in the world—to prove what is true and expose what is false. Trials verify God's power, confirm His nature, and validate His reality. They also reveal God's dominion over chaotic situations. Isaiah 43:2 says, *"When you pass through the waters, I will be with you; and through the rivers, they shall not overflow* [overwhelm] *you. When you walk through the fire, you shall not be burned, nor shall the flame scorch you"* (NKJV).

> Trials verify God's power, confirm His nature, and validate His reality.

Trials are similar to tests in that a person who undergoes a trial may experience pain or anguish that tries his patience, endurance, or belief. Trials are very personal to the individual involved. It is essential to recognize, however, that God's sovereignty is the context of every biblical trial, even though individuals may be tested in the midst of them. Let's look at several examples of biblical trials.

The Israelites at the Red Sea

After the nation of Israel left Egypt and set out for the Promised Land, the Egyptian army pursued them. They were caught between this mighty army and the Red Sea, with seemingly no way out. This was a perilous situation, the main purpose of which was to reveal the glory and power of God over those who would destroy His people. God saved the Israelites by causing the sea to part and holding it up on both sides so that they could cross safely to the other shore. The Egyptians followed them but were drowned as the seas came crashing down upon them. (See Exodus 14:5-27.) God's people went through a trial that validated their faith in almighty God, confirmed His nature, and illustrated His sovereignty over the enemy.

The Israelites' Entrance into the Promised Land

In order for the nation of Israel to enter into the Promised Land, they had to cross the Jordan River. When they reached it, its banks were flooded, as they always were during harvest season. God told His people to cross the swollen river. The priests were to carry the ark of the covenant ahead of the people, and God would again part the waters to enable them to get to the other side. The Bible says that the Israelites approached the river by faith with the ark of the covenant ahead of them, just as God had told them to do. When the feet of the priests touched the edge of the river, the waters parted, and the people crossed over safely. (See Joshua 3:7-17.) Their faith in the living God was confirmed, and the power and glory of God were visible to all.

Jesus' Calming of the Storm

Jesus had told His disciples to travel by boat to the other side of the Sea of Galilee while He dismissed the large crowd that had gathered to hear His teaching. He would join them later on. When the disciples were about halfway across the water, a bad storm blew in and strong winds threatened the boat. During the night, Jesus came to them, walking on the water. As soon as He stepped into the boat, the wind immediately stopped. The disciples' reaction was to worship Jesus, saying, *"Of a truth thou art the Son of God"* (Matthew 14:33). This incident was a test of the disciples' faith, and it glorified God by demonstrating His power over nature and revealing the identity of His Son. (See Matthew 14:22–33.)

Jesus' Passion

Jesus underwent severe trial when He died for our sins on the cross. This trial sharply tested Jesus' obedience to the Father. First, He was falsely accused of blasphemy and treason, taken from one judgment hall to another, and interrogated by both religious and civil authorities. His identity, integrity, and innocence were questioned. Second, He was severely punished, even though He was innocent of all charges brought against Him. Third, He was put to death in a devastatingly cruel way before being resurrected by the Father. (See John 18:1–20:18.)

His passion, that is, His season of trial, began with false accusations, continued with His death and burial, and ended with His triumphant resurrection. The authorities and many others had doubted His authenticity and power to do what He said He would do. Yet He was tried by the fire of His experience and declared to be King of kings and Lord of lords. His obedience in enduring the cross brought glory to God and revealed His power over sin and death.

The Sufferings of Our Fallen World

We will all go through tests and trials because, through them, our faith is perfected and God's glory is revealed to the world. In addition, because sin entered our world when the first man and woman disobeyed God, we will always go through some measure of pain and suffering in this life. It is natural to have some doubt and confusion when we experience difficulties. Yet our ultimate response to our troubles will either bring glory to God or reveal that we haven't truly learned to love and trust Him. In this sense, everything we go through is a trial of faith.

> **Everything we go through is a trial of faith.**

The Answer to Our Pain

Jesus understands that we will experience difficult times. He said, *"In this world you will have trouble. But take heart! I have overcome the world"* (John 16:33 NIV). One of the ways Jesus has overcome the world is that He is able to heal us of the wounds that the world inflicts on us. Again, the Bible says that Jesus came to heal *all manner* of conditions:

> *And Jesus went about all Galilee, teaching in their syna-gogues, preaching the gospel of the kingdom, and healing all kinds of sickness and all kinds of disease among the people. Then His fame went throughout all Syria; and they brought to Him all sick people who were afflicted with various dis-eases and torments, and those who were demon-possessed, epileptics, and paralytics; and He healed them.*
>
> (Matthew 4:23–24 NKJV)

Through the power of the Holy Spirit, an anointing is available to bring you the good news of your deliverance, bind up your broken heart, and free you from the confinement of your negative experiences—mending your wounds while removing the evidential scars from your life.

"If the Son therefore shall make you free, ye shall be free indeed" (John 8:36). Invariably, each time Jesus healed someone, He delivered that person from some behavioral manifestation of the sickness as well as from the sickness itself. There was always some level of healing in the individual's way of life: a beggar's coat that must be cast away by a blind man; a withered hand, which had been obvious to others, that must now be stretched out in front of the same crowd; a bed that must be taken up and carried, rather than be lain upon. (See, for example, Mark 10:46–52; Luke 6:6–10; John 5:5–9.) All these examples speak of God's power to heal and deliver you from the mind-set and emotional evidence related to your hurtful experiences.

Jesus knows and understands that you may have developed a relationship with grief, just as those whom He healed had settled into pain as a way of life before they encountered Him. Pain, rejection, or disappointment can become a constant companion. You may have deep wounds that are the result of turning to those who should have received you and finding that, like your enemies, they also turn away.

Jesus wants to carry the weight of your experience. Remember that He has taken your place: He was wounded so that you would not have to be wounded any longer. He was bruised so that you could be healed of self-defeating habits. The wounds on His back were inflicted to heal you of the wounds and scars in your life. Jesus has already paid the price for your pain. He joins you now in the furnace of your experience, whether it is a test, a trial, or the sufferings inflicted by a fallen world. *"Lo, I see four men loose, walking in the midst of the fire, and they have no hurt; and the form of the fourth is like the Son of God"* (Daniel 3:25).

Chapter Four

Removing the Mask

*The masks we create for ourselves conceal our pain
but prevent our healing.*

Even when we understand that God desires to heal our wounds and scars, we often prevent our own deliverance by blocking the healing process. For too long, many of us have tried to deal with our pain by hiding behind a false impression of correctness, competence, self-confidence, or spirituality. This is the reason why we have missed the deliverance that God promises us. We wear masks of supposed peace and joy. Outwardly, we praise and worship God as though we have never been wounded, much less scarred. Our goal is to try to conceal the truth of our pain from both others and ourselves.

Before we can be healed, we must remove our masks. We have to be honest about our past as well as our feelings about our negative experiences and the effect that they have had on our lives. At times, all of us wear masks of one kind or another. I hope that the story of Tracey will clearly demonstrate what masks do to us and how we can be healed only by removing them and allowing God to transform us into who we were truly created to be.

Having It All Together

Tracey was one of those people who appear to have it all together. She was dressed impeccably as she sat next to me in her first-class airline seat. As we talked, I recognized that she was also articulate, aggressive, accomplished, and upwardly mobile. Her image was well-scrubbed, well-polished, and practiced. I was traveling first class that day because they had needed a seat in coach. I began to realize that my being moved up was not for my comfort alone. It was also for Tracey's deliverance.

As she spoke about her life, she was careful not to reveal anything personal about herself. She never talked about anything except her company and the next city that she would invade. Her words were well-structured as she explained the nature of her employment and what it was like to travel the country downsizing divisions of her company. She was a "hatchet woman" who seemed to enjoy her job. In essence, she made her living by putting other people out of work. Her longevity at her job was due to her ability to make her company money by reducing payroll while increasing the productivity of the "survivors."

> Before we can be healed, we must remove our masks.

Running, Not Pursuing

"By the sound of things, you should be very happy," I said. Her expression changed, and I could see doubt mixed in with her display of confidence. As our conversation progressed, it became clear that she was not mercenary by nature but had developed a hardened outer shell to survive the tough business environment she had to operate in. Living by cell phone, she was always working, and she traveled continually. She mentioned that she exercised seven days a week, in whatever city she was in, usually just before collapsing into bed at the end of the day.

"You seem to be running, not pursuing," I observed, and I saw fear in her eyes. The outlook of a person who is pursuing a goal is remarkably different from the mind-set of a person who is running from something. She bristled, shut down, and suddenly had an intense interest in the magazine selection in front of her. She appeared to be insulted by my comment but intrigued at the same time. I waited. About an hour went by before she spoke again and asked me what I meant.

I explained to Tracey that it was clear she was running away from herself. The image that she was trying to project was not who she appeared to me to be. For one thing, she was dressed in a way that neutralized her femininity. She had sacrificed her femaleness at the corporate altar in order to gain acceptance and upward mobility. I noticed that she was not wearing any jewelry, and I remarked how difficult it must be to maintain relationships with her demanding schedule.

She began to recite a practiced litany, expressing her disinterest and lack of need for relationships of any kind. Her tone of voice became extremely edgy as she pushed very hard to press her point. Time did not allow for any kind of relationship, she said. Besides, all the men she met were insecure about her success. They didn't understand her goals and aspirations. A traditional relationship was something she didn't need or want. Her remarks were accompanied by all the appropriate dismissive gestures and facial expressions. She finally stopped her monologue and asked me what I thought. I simply said, "I don't believe you." Her mouth dropped open.

I asked Tracey how long she had been running from her pain. The practiced expression dissolved and tears welled up in her eyes. Her facade as an uncaring and unfeeling corporate hatchet began to crumble—but she fought for control harder than anyone I have ever seen. There was nowhere to run, so she looked out the window. Then she asked me, "Are you some kind of counselor or something?"

"No," I answered, "just someone who works with people for a living." I told her that goals were fine if they were a choice, but it was obvious that her goals were an escape from herself. I am still not sure why I asked her the next question. I don't know whether it was mere curiosity or inspiration, but there was something that she had said about working out right before going to bed that gave me some insight. I asked her how often she cried herself to sleep.

A Wound Revisited

She looked at me incredulously and asked, "How did you know?" I had located the wound. The remains of the mask of her professional image disintegrated. She began to talk about a relationship that had started in college and led to marriage.

She had held all the normal aspirations, setting her sights on a home, children, a nice neighborhood, and a fulfilling career. She made the decision to postpone her career plans to work two jobs so that her husband could complete the postgraduate work necessary to put them in a strong financial position. She would get her advanced degree after he got his.

She was committed to her husband, so the arrangement made sense. She worked hard, pushing her desire for children and career aside. He graduated, obtained a plum position, and began to make a name for himself.

In college, she and her husband had always been peers professionally and intellectually, but slowly his perception of her had begun to shift. At first, he expressed impatience toward her. Then hostility concerning her lack of professional development crept into his conversation. (His reaction didn't make any sense to me, either.) As the months passed, she began to isolate herself from everyone, hiding the problem from her parents and friends. She feared that people would be able to see beneath the cover she was using to disguise her failing marriage. She tried everything she knew to plug the damage in the leaking ship she called a relationship, but nothing worked. Her husband came home late one night and announced that he was leaving and filing for divorce. Now her dreams for her life totally slipped away. Her emotions evolved from shattered to hopeless, from angry to outraged. She determined that this would never happen to her again. To accomplish this goal, she began to create an elaborate mask.

Tracey could have moved home with her parents, but that would have been a constant reminder of her failure. Her family had its expectations. Failure was not an option even if she was unhappy. A fifteen-minute explanation of the situation was all she gave her mother and father. She told them that her husband was gone, that she was sorry they were disappointed, and that she would, of course, be fine. Her mother seemed to have no understanding of marital failure while her father simply said that he had never liked the guy anyway. Neither was much help. Tracey couldn't tell if their eyes held pity or compassion. That was the last time she had talked about her divorce to anyone until she sat next to me on the airplane.

After her husband left, Tracey dove into her work and went to school at night. She had always been driven by the expectations of others, so she covered over all her pain and disappointment with achievement, titles, and an uncaring attitude. As she moved up the corporate ladder, she left corporate corpses in her wake. She was proud of the fact that she never missed a day of work, but every night she would cry. The hurt she felt inside made it easier to do her job because she was hardening her heart to those around her. Eventually, the Tracey in the mirror began to obscure the woman on the inside.

The mask was so complete that her friends had given up trying to help her. Tracey was a stranger to the people who knew her. She allowed no one to get close enough to hurt her. If she felt a new friendship developing, she immediately withdrew. She always found a fault in the other person that was significant enough to validate her hostility. In this way, she created a safety zone around her feelings.

> She had always been driven by others' expectations.

A Type of Death

Divorce has been described as a type of death. It is the death of a relationship, the termination of a close family unit, and is potentially fatal to the emotions. Its effects are lingering. Some people never completely recover from the experience. They enter new relationships with gaping wounds and deep scars and find it difficult to establish permanent bonds. In fact, the emotional response to divorce is remarkably similar to the emotional response to abuse. There is often either gross indiscretion—in which a person enters into many intimate encounters seeking assurance that he or she is desirable—or else complete relational shutdown. Both are attempts to exercise protective control over the emotions.

Sexual Indiscretion

Gross indiscretion is usually acted out as a promiscuous season in a person's life. The individual often justifies this season by telling himself or herself, "I'm just doing what I want to do." In reality, it is an attempt to take charge of all present and future relationships. Sometimes, the attachment may masquerade as a full relationship, but it is usually nothing more than a physical one. It looks like a relationship, but it's just a facade. There is no real intimacy because that would require commitment and vulnerability.

The lifestyle accompanying this season of indiscretion is often one of partying and hanging out with groups of people who are doing the same thing. This temporarily mutes any guilt or shame the person may be feeling about the indiscretion, and it also deceives him or her into believing that one can enter into physical relationships without experiencing any emotional ties. These casual attachments involve no real commitment, but the consequence is permanent damage to the person's self-image. One set of emotions appears to be protected, but the entire emotional framework is being devastated because the person becomes profoundly disappointed with the person he or she is becoming. Attention, money, and social activity are weak compensations for the loss of self-esteem.

Emotional Shutdown

The other extreme is a complete shutdown in relation to emotional involvement. When a person is feeling hurt, disappointed, and discarded, he or she may decide that the safest place to be is in a fortress of emotional self-exile. Finding solace in activities, work, and even parenting, the person pulls back from everything that looks like an emotional commitment. There appears to be safety in isolation, but the issues causing the isolation are never resolved.

Controlled by the Past

Seasons of indiscretion and self-exile are masks that people use to hide their hurt. Tracey was having a hybrid season that included elements of both. Most of the time, she would sequester herself in her work, but from time to time (and these times were becoming more frequent), she would enter into indiscretion. She was involved in brief physical relationships, usually when she was out of town. These people would never intersect with the mainstream of her life so she could protect her feelings. Her emotions were raging like a storm, but she kept them behind her mask.

I asked Tracey how long she intended to let her ex-husband control her life. She bristled and explained that the facade she had created and the things that she was doing had nothing to do with him. I let her finish, waiting to ask the question that would begin her deliverance. "At what point in your life do you first remember feeling the way you do?" She hesitated. I persisted, "If your relationship had been successful, would you feel the way you do?"

I did not wait for an answer. It was obvious that she was not free from her ex-husband because she was still reacting to him. He was still in control of her life. Everything she did was to prove that she could make it without him and that she was desirable to other men.

A New Purpose in Life

Tracey thought that the mask covering her emotions was complete, but her eyes had revealed her pain to me. The eyes are the windows of our experience, and it is impossible to fully hide behind them. They reveal joy, peace, and contentment, but they also betray fear, disappointment, and bitterness.

It was clear to me that Tracey was driven by the wounds of her divorce. This was reflected in the scars of her behavior. She needed the Good Shepherd to heal her and bring her into a place of peace. I knew that her moment of deliverance had arrived, and I began to offer her hope through Jesus Christ.

The underlying cause of Tracey's brokenness was that she had lost sight of her true reason for living. In fact, she had never known it. Through talking with her, I had discovered that she had been raised in a moral home, but one that did not acknowledge God. Her unspoken idea of success was to emulate the stoic marriage of her parents. I explained to her that God had a purpose for her life and that understanding this purpose was essential to her healing. Her purpose for herself had been to have a relationship with her ex-husband. All her dreams had been wrapped up in him. That is why, when the relationship failed, she had felt lost.

> Understanding God's purpose is essential to our healing.

Release through Forgiveness

I explained that her ultimate fulfillment would be found in the Lord and that God's eternal purpose included her survival in the adversities of life. Her reaction to her divorce had been incorrect, but she had survived. She was wounded and scarred by her experience, but there was hope. She no longer needed to hide from herself. Then I asked her if she'd forgiven her husband for leaving her. "I will never forgive him," she said. "Then he will always be in control of your life," I replied.

Forgiveness is a release. When Jesus said, "Father, forgive them, because they have no idea what they are doing," God ceased to hold the sin against those who put His Son to death. (See Luke 23:33–34.) I explained to Tracey that if she didn't forgive her husband, it would be as if she were tied to him by a rope for the rest of her life.

She explained how much she had done for him in putting him through school. All the things that she had sacrificed poured out of her again. She had obviously repeated this litany to herself. It was well rehearsed and punctuated with all the anger and resentment that she could muster. When she was finished, I told her that she had a right to be angry but that her anger was not affecting him one way or another. She was wasting her anger on him when she should be angry with herself for allowing him to control her life.

> **The Man she needed first and foremost was Jesus.**

The greatest insult was not the fact that he had left her. It was that she was still holding on to him with her anger long after he was gone. The real Tracey was lost behind her nonproductive responses to her pain. She had the right idea. The empty space in her heart did need to be filled. However, in her attempt to fill the void, she'd made the wrong decisions and connected to the wrong people and situations.

The Man she needed first and foremost was Jesus. It was time to remove the mask and allow Him to heal her. I asked her if she was interested in feeling differently than she felt right now. Then I asked her to pray with me, and she agreed. As we made our way through a confession of faith and of receiving Christ as Savior, I turned the prayer into a prayer of forgiveness for her husband. I called him her husband because he was still affecting her emotionally. She had not yet released him.

When we reached the forgiveness part of the prayer, she hesitated. We waited at the crossroads of her deliverance. She pressed her way through, finally saying the words, "I forgive him." Her shoulders slumped and tears fell like rain down her face. She looked up, and I could see that the anger was gone. The weight of her negative experience and bitterness had been lifted.

I began to remind her of the good things in her life that had come about after her divorce. She had vocational success. She had become self-reliant, proving to herself that she could make it, if she had to, on her own. If she hadn't gone through her difficulties, she would have missed our meeting that day on the plane. Perhaps she would not have come to salvation in Christ without undergoing her tragic experience.

God was at work in Tracey's life despite her negative circumstances. Through His power, the mask she had created was removed. She rediscovered her real self, and her wounded heart was healed.

Have You Discovered Your True Self?

Have you been hiding behind a mask in order to conceal your pain, fear, or disappointment? Is there a person everyone knows and a person within you who remains a secret?

One of the great tragedies of life is that many people feel the need to put on a good external appearance or demonstrate political correctness, despite their true circumstances or feelings.

We face this type of pressure in our jobs, in our relationships, and even in the church. No one likes to feel the vulnerability that comes with being transparent. In an attempt to protect ourselves, we forge an identity that we think will be acceptable to people. At the same time, however, we risk obscuring who we really are—who God created us to be. With practice, it becomes as easy to convey the impression that we desire to project as it is to put on a new outfit of clothes. We put on what we think will accomplish our mission on a particular day.

Part of our dilemma is that we are all too aware of our unflattering character traits, and we don't want others to recognize them. Instead of facing our need for change, we manufacture a false personality, an image that we hope is appealing.

> **We obscure who we really are—who God created us to be.**

As a result, each relationship we enter into brings both a sweet and sour taste to our lives. The enjoyment of a new relationship is always mixed with the fear of discovery. Externally, we are excited, while inwardly, we wait for the negative characteristics of our personalities or pasts to be uncovered. On the one hand, we hope someone will come along who is willing to accept the "unacceptable" parts of our lives. On the other hand, we anticipate an all-too-familiar rejection.

Because we tie our worth to others' acceptance of us, our identities actually change according to the particular situations and people we encounter. In this way, our identities become fractured.

An Assumed Character

The problem with developing masks to hide our true selves from others is that we end up trying to hide from God, as well. Jesus referred to the Pharisees as those who operated their lives behind masks. He called them *"hypocrites."* (See, for example, Matthew 15:7; Luke 11:44.) One meaning of the Greek word for *hypocrite* is "an actor under an assumed character (stage-player)." (See *Strong's*, #G5273.)

The Pharisees of Jesus' day were experts at creating and sustaining masks of respectability. They were skilled at playing a part that appealed to the public, giving the impression that they were more spiritual than they actually were. They were posturing to impress. Jesus called them sepulchers painted white. While they appeared to be pure on the outside, death and decay were on the inside. (See Matthew 23:27.) He also called them *"blind guides"* (vv. 16, 24). They claimed an ability to lead that they did not possess.

> The facades we create can dominate our lives.

If we are not careful, the facades that we create for ourselves will begin to dominate our day-to-day existence, just as they did for the Pharisees. Then, when a new emotional experience or intense circumstance forces the wounds and scars of the past to the surface of our lives, we will experience great internal tension. We will desire to be free from the hurt, but we will be afraid to reveal the pain. When we pray about our situations, we will wear our masks into the presence of God, and therefore we won't experience any release. Then we will wonder if God is paying any attention to us at all.

Dropping the Mask

Have you often wondered if God is aware of your pain? He is. Yet deliverance cannot occur until you drop the mask in His presence. Pretence in the presence of God will hinder your release because a mask is often a tool of denial, which is another roadblock to deliverance. It is impossible to experience true freedom without real confession, and confession cannot happen in the face of denial. In the New Testament, the word *confess* means "to acknowledge or agree fully." (See *Strong's*, #G1843.)

Genuine confession agrees with God that the pain and its causes are real. You may need to confess how you contributed to your scars, either by willing disobedience or unforgiveness toward those who have hurt you, such as in Tracey's situation. Being fully cleansed of the toxicity of negative experiences can happen only when you are honest with God. When you confess your pain, you offer it to Him as a sacrifice; you release it to Him. The Bible says, *"Casting all your care upon him; for he careth for you"* (1 Peter 5:7).

No More Pain

The tragic scenes of your life have been vividly replayed in your heart and mind long enough. The reality of these circumstances cannot be erased, but the pain, wounds, and scars can be. God wants to heal your wounds and remove your scars so that you can say, "I remember it, but it doesn't hurt anymore."

Shadrach, Meshach, and Abednego could never deny the reality of their furnace experience. It happened to them. The danger of death and the fear and dread of the furnace were real. As I wrote earlier, the emotional impact of being in a place where they should have died should have had a long-lasting emotional impact on them. The memory of the flames should have produced nightmares and a need for some form of therapy. The sight of fire should have produced flashbacks, crippling them emotionally and psychologically. Yet the men came out of the fire without a hair on their heads being singed or the smell of smoke on their bodies. The total negative impact of the experience was taken away by the presence and power of God. They had no lingering effects of a season in their lives that the enemy thought would destroy them. They had the memory of it, but no pain connected with it.

God wants to do the same thing for you. It really is time to remove the mask and let Him into the hottest part of your pain so that you can be healed. The presence of God can transform any circumstance. If you will drop your mask and trust your heavenly Father, Jesus will enter the furnace of your negative season and deliver you from the destructive fires of hurt and shame.

Chapter Five

Faithful God and Father

Your deliverance will come from the realization that what your parents lacked in raising you is a revelation of what God desires to be in your life.

My father was a disappointment to me in many ways. The label *father* was really an inappropriate title for him because he never really wanted to be one. In chapter two, I talked about his problems with substance abuse. I remember him sitting on the sofa in starched pants and a pressed shirt, drinking and becoming more sullen as the day continued. His words were few, void of encouragement, and usually sarcastic.

A Father's Absence

After my parents split up, I lived with my mother in west Philadelphia on Angora Terrace. Angora was one of those unusually quiet inner-city streets. When you turned on to it, you slipped into another dimension. It was lined with big Sycamore trees, there were no piles of trash, the hedges were meticulously clipped, and the four-foot-square patches of front lawn were neatly cut and edged.

One day, I took the bus to visit my father at his apartment in another part of town. It was a sunny day, and as I rode through the streets of the city, the noise, music, and smells of the neighborhoods changed with the prevailing ethnic presence. My stop was Sixtieth and Market. I got off and walked to Fifty-eighth.

The residences along Market Street were unique. Elevated train tracks ran down the center of the road. From Sixtieth to Fifty-eighth, the well-kept storefronts formed a chain of urban enterprise. An apartment was above each store. These apartments, mostly on the second floor but some on the third, had a wonderful view of the tracks. The train rumbled down the street every few minutes, shaking everything it passed, with its shadow crossing over the sunny side of the street.

My dad's place was on the sunny side. I arrived at the pink storefront of the furniture business that was underneath his apartment. The store's door was so narrow that I wondered how they got the furniture inside. I knocked. Dad was always home at this time of the afternoon because he worked at night. He had one of those jobs where you could drink. He slept most of the day, then got up in the afternoon to watch TV and start drinking gin all over again.

The man who owned the store answered my knock and asked whom I was looking for. He told me that my father had moved away. He didn't know where, but he had been gone for at least a month.

My father had left without a word. I retraced my steps through the Market Street neighborhood, caught the bus home, and walked back to my house without noticing anything around me. My mother asked, "Why are you home so early?" I simply said, "He moved." The last time I had seen my father was a month earlier, and I never saw him again.

Everything about my life was clouded by my father's absence. As the years went by, I won sports races and matches without his affirmation. Graduation after graduation, achievement after achievement, I heard nothing from him. The missing praise and encouragement that every child needs left a gap within me that needed to be filled. I developed a wound that felt as if it would never heal. This wound turned into a scar. Feeling abandoned and forsaken, I assumed that most fathers were like mine.

After about twenty years, I began to feel a need to see my father. Looking back, I realize that it was the Holy Spirit who was leading me to ask my brother to go with me to visit our father in South Carolina. We made plans to go, but our schedules delayed the trip one weekend. During the delay, our father died.

The news of his death had no immediate effect on me. Then guilt crept over me because I wasn't feeling what I thought I should feel. Had the years without a relationship with my father produced a scarring so thick that I was unable to experience the appropriate feelings of grief? I thought that I should have cried many tears and mourned many days, and I asked God for an explanation about what was going on inside me.

I began to understand that, as the years had passed, my father's absence had removed all but the slightest expectations that I had originally had for him. Any hopes of a relationship had long ceased. When my mother gave me the news of his passing, I remember that I shed only one tear. That tear represented my sadness over what could have been but never was.

Presence and Relationship

There are two main things that people grieve over when a father passes away. First, they miss his continual presence or availability to them. Second, they miss the bond of relationship that they have shared over the years, with all its facets, such as love, companionship, counsel, and humor. If these elements of family connectedness were weak or nonexistent in your own parental relationship, you may feel that there is little to mourn when your parent dies. If you didn't have the benefit of an affirming father, you may process his passing in a way that seems unusual, such as the lack of grief that I experienced. It is unfair to compare your feelings to the feelings of someone who had a very strong, caring relationship with his father and who experienced his father's affirmation. If a father has a positive relationship with his children, he gives them something to truly miss when he is gone.

This doesn't mean that you won't experience certain feelings of loss if an absentee father dies. Someone once said that "you can't miss what you can't measure." Yet my experience and the experiences of others confirm that you *can* miss what you can't measure. Your missing out on a loving parental relationship can leave gaping emotional wounds and deep scars. Let's take a closer look at why this is so.

Expectations of Our Earthly Fathers

Many people harbor disappointment connected to their parents'—particularly their fathers'—inability to fulfill their expectations. Regardless of how old or young we are, we have a list of assumptions, needs, hopes, and disappointments associated with the title *father*. This is because a father is a child's first hero. He is the knight in shining armor who can do no wrong in the sight of young, innocent eyes.

A father is expected to be many things, such as protector, mediator, and intercessor—sensing our needs and always able to supply them. When life wounds us, he is the one that we want to run to. We turn to him as a present help in difficulty. A father is also expected to be a friend and advisor—guiding us through the maze of life with wisdom and understanding. He is a living example of adulthood, and we often emulate his gestures, activities, aspirations, and moods. Whether or not our particular fathers are—or were—qualified to fulfill these roles, most of us at least start out with these (conscious or subconscious) expectations of them.

> A father is expected to be a child's hero, friend, and advisor.

Expectation versus Reality

I think that most fathers have a desire to be good parents. If this is the case, then why have many of our fathers disappointed or failed us? They simply lacked the tools to follow through on what they believed that a father should be. For example, consider a man who is constantly making promises to his child that he fails to keep. His child may eventually think of him as unreliable and even a liar. Yet the fact that he makes promises may be an indication of his desire to do a better job. Paul said, in effect, "The will is in me, but the trouble comes in not being able to get it done." (See Romans 7:18.)

Our emotional struggles often start as we mature and begin to take a more realistic view of our fathers than we had as small children. Our positive perception of them lies in their ability to follow through on their promises and fulfill our hopes for them—whether we have expressed these hopes or not. As promises and expectations are met, our confidence and trust in them is built. When they are broken or left unfulfilled, we become disappointed. With each new disappointment, wounds are created. In time, scars develop. In order to survive, we discard our expectations as a method of emotional survival. If our fathers have been physically absent from our lives, their presence and confirming voice becomes less important to us as the years progress—at least, that's what we tell ourselves. This emotional distancing from our fathers is not the heart's desire—it is the mind's attempt to protect the heart.

Substitutes for the Father's Presence

When our fathers are absent, we have difficulty maturing emotionally as we grow to adulthood. As we experience one important milestone after the next and accomplish both ordinary and extraordinary achievements, we may experience an intense emptiness that often grows rather than diminishes as we get older. This emptiness must be filled. Therefore, as the pain of the loss becomes more intense and the scars begin to crowd our emotions, we look for substitutes for our fathers' presence.

There is no substitute for a father's affirmation.

The voices that present themselves as alternatives—sexual indiscretion, substance abuse, workaholism, to name a few—are deceptive. They promise a degree of comfort and fulfillment, and they give a glimpse of hope, but they never satisfy our basic need for the affirmation of a father.

"The Power of Death and Life"

One of the reasons a father's role is so significant is that he has been given a powerful tool of influence—his "voice." Among the greatest gifts—and responsibilities—that God has given humanity is the power of our words. This is part of our creation in His image. God accomplishes His will and purpose through His words. In Genesis 1, we read that when the Creator said, *"Let there be…,"* He transformed the darkness and gave shape and order to a world without form. Every dimension of our natural environment came into being through His words. Likewise, mankind, who is created in God's image, was designed to exercise dominion on the earth by using words as an instrument of authority. Recall that the first specific task that God gave Adam was to name all the animals. (See Genesis 2:19–20.)

> One of the greatest gifts that God has given humanity is the power of our words.

Referring to the force of words, the Bible says that *"death and life are in the power of the tongue"* (Proverbs 18:21). All people influence others by their words. Yet when a man speaks according to the Spirit of God, he has tremendous power, and his words will stand. For instance, when the patriarch Jacob was dying, he called his sons to his bedside, and he prophesied concerning what would happen to the tribes of Israel that would descend from them. His words either committed them to greatness or exacted judgment. The voice of Jacob affected the future of his children's children.

Whether or not a father is speaking according to God's Spirit, his words have a special potency. He has the ability to hinder his children's futures or to encourage them to greater achievement by what he says to them. The parent who derides his child after a failure or defeat sows destruction, but the parent who gives his child hope after failure, removing the pain from defeat, sows life. Having an affirming parental voice is an essential part of our wholeness.

The Effects of Rejection

The point that I have been leading up to is that disappointment and pain associated with our fathers can have a very serious spiritual outcome: It can have a crippling effect on our relationships with God. We often think of God in terms of what our fathers were like. If we were unable to trust our fathers, we may have difficulty trusting God. This lack of understanding or trust in God as Father not only adds to our emotional pain, but also hinders us from allowing Him to heal the wounds and scars in our lives. We can't or won't enter God's presence for healing if we aren't sure how He will treat us.

> We often think of God in terms of what our fathers were like.

For a vivid illustration of how a parental relationship can influence a person's relationship with God, let's look at the tragic results of poor fathering in the life of Michal, the daughter of Saul, first king of Israel.

Michal's father is a king, yet she still needs him to be her parent. His title does not eliminate his responsibility to be her protector and nurturer. Yet Saul is unpredictable. He vacillates between rage and love, murderous fits of anger and calm. He appears to cherish his children, but then uses them for political collateral. Reading between the lines of the biblical text in 1 and 2 Samuel, I imagine that Michal loves her father but has experienced rejection and insecurity from an early age. When she enters her father's presence, she has no idea which Saul she will face. She and her siblings never know whether he will embrace them or rage at them.

Then a young shepherd named David comes into the family's life. After David kills the Philistine enemy Goliath, Saul rewards him by putting him in charge of a thousand soldiers and reaffirming his promise to give him his daughter, Merab, as his wife. Saul, however, becomes insecure about his position when he sees David's popularity with the soldiers and people of Israel. David even has the admiration of Saul's own servants.

Saul goes back on his promise and gives Merab to another man in marriage. Then he finds out that Michal is in love with David. He sees her love as an opportunity to achieve his own political agenda—getting rid of his supposed competitor. Although a father should protect the heart of his daughter, Saul sets her up for heartbreak. He wants to use her to help entrap and kill the one she loves. A true father would try to preserve his daughter's happiness, not destroy it.

Saul sets up his scheme by promising Michal to David. Let's look at the situation from Michal's point of view. She is getting married! It would be a ceremony fit for a princess. She is appropriately excited and experiences all the dreams of a bride. But Saul has decided that her wedding will be David's funeral. Michal is an object of exploitation. Saul loves her only for what he can get from her.

I imagine that Saul grows even more aggravated with the situation when he realizes that the honor and admiration that he desires from Michal is going to David, instead. Michal is not alone. Her brother, Jonathan, also shifts his loyalty and admiration to David. Both children find what they need in another individual. When a child is continually rejected by a parent, he or she will find someone or something to fill the void that the rejection has caused. David is hero, leader, and strength to Michal, and he is brother, friend, and confidant to Jonathan.

Michal might have been happy with David. Yet since all she has known is her father's undependability, she is not equipped for a relationship with her new husband. I think that this element contributes in a large way to what happens to her in the end. Rejection will rob you of the strengths necessary for relationship.

At first, Michal resists her father by fighting for David's life. She finds out what Saul is planning and helps David to escape. She is in an awful position. She has been forced to give up her father in an emotional sense, and now she must give up her beloved husband to keep him from being killed.

Notice that Michal helps David to get away, but she doesn't go with him. Why did she stay behind? I think that she stayed because all she has experienced up to now is rejection. Pushing people away is all she knows. The thought of going with David never crosses her mind. Subconsciously, she expects David to reject her as Saul has.

People who have been wounded by undependable relationships often set themselves up for additional wounding. Giving and receiving love becomes very difficult. Their expectations of rejection become self-fulfilling prophecies: They act negatively toward others until they force those who care about them to reject them. Then they tell themselves, "I knew that they would never hang around."

Michal's situation gets even worse. As if Saul has not done enough to hurt her, he gives her to another man to be his wife. She is married to David, but he gives her to Phalti. Michal is put into a compromising situation that her father should have protected her from.

Fourteen years go by. Saul and Jonathan are killed in battle, and David becomes king of Judah. Soon he will become king of all Israel, and as one of his negotiating points, he demands Michal back. But note what has happened during those intervening years. Phalti truly loves Michal. Someone finally loves her for her own sake, and she is taken from him. The Bible says that, as she is led away, Phalti follows her for a long time, weeping. Perhaps Michal cried, but the Bible never records her shedding a tear.

I imagine that Michal left without a word or show of emotion. Rejection and disappointment have hardened her heart. She has been damaged by life. Her wounds began with her father, and they reached their summit with David.

Later, David brings the ark of the covenant back to Jerusalem. It has been absent from the city for many years after being captured by the Philistines. David and the people are celebrating its return and praising God, and Michal is in the window of the palace observing this procession. David is so wrapped up in his worship of God that he is leaping and dancing. Yet instead of joining in the celebration, Michal *"despised him in her heart"* (2 Samuel 6:16). When David comes into the palace to bless his family, Michal bitterly and sarcastically criticizes him.

> Repeated rejection can harden your heart to praise and the presence of God.

Repeated rejection can harden your heart to praise and the presence of God. Michal is wounded. Emotional abuse has blocked both her natural and spiritual sensitivities. She has a right to be disappointed (though her ultimate reaction to her disappointment was sinful and spiritually destructive). There is no record of the men in her life coming to her assistance. Also, the Bible records no infraction on her part when she was a young girl. She was not a disobedient daughter, selfish sister, or untrustworthy person in her early years. She was not rejected by her father because of any negative characteristic. She had virtue. Nothing was wrong with her; something was wrong with Saul. What was missing in Michal's life was the fellowship, validation, and confirmation of her father. She needed Saul to say, "This is my beloved daughter, in whom I am well pleased." She also needed his protection. Instead, her father rejected her, used her, tore apart her marriage, and abused her emotions. Consequently, she didn't trust anyone.

Michal also seems to have come to distrust God, even though He had done nothing to her. The Bible describes Michal as barren. Something inside her is dead. She is locked in a prison of rejection. Her anger toward David *feels* right, yet the venom she releases is sin, and sin kills praise and fellowship with God. (See 1 Samuel 17:32–19:17; 25:44; 2 Samuel 2:1–4; 3:1–16; 5:1–3; 6:1–23.)

Overcoming Disappointment and Hurt

To a greater or lesser degree, all of us live with disappointment over the way our fathers raised us (or failed to raise us). We were created for a relationship with a father. It is in our makeup to need and respond to a father's guidance and care. When that relationship is injured, we experience personal brokenness. What is the key to our healing? How can we deal with our hurt, as well as the devastating effect it can have on our relationships with God? Let me share with you what I have learned over the years as God has patiently dealt with me concerning this issue. Think about your own relationship with your father and see if lost expectations may be hindering the healing you seek.

Your Father Was Not Superman

First, recognize that your father was not superman. He possessed the same strengths and weaknesses common to others. Your deliverance from feelings of rejection and disappointment will come from knowing that your father was probably all he could be at the time. Your desire that he be something he's demonstrated he isn't has created a stronghold in your emotions. You will continually experience anger and disappointment if you keep expecting your father to be something that he has no ability—or desire—to be.

It is sometimes difficult for us to let go of the expectations of childhood. Yet if you hold on to them, you will just increase your anger and resentment because, each time you see your father, you will keep looking for a change in him. Again, don't expect him to be something that he cannot be. Release your anger. Forgive him for his weaknesses and for the pain that he has caused you—whether it was intentional or unintentional. Allow yourself to move on in your life.

The Weakness of Your Earthly Father Highlights the Strength of Your Heavenly Father

Second, understand that, in God's original design, our earthly fathers were meant to represent the fatherhood of God. It should be the goal of every father to pass along his positive strengths and wisdom to his children. Our lives are not lived entirely for the present. We are producing a legacy that our descendants and others whom we influence will remember and be affected by. It is a legacy of either honor or dishonor that they will cherish or regret.

While our fathers may fail to represent the heavenly Father, the fact remains that God is always a true Father to us. He loves us as His own children. *"Behold, what manner of love the Father hath bestowed upon us, that we should be called the sons of God"* (1 John 3:1).

An amazing spiritual revelation can occur when our fathers fail us. Through our disappointment in them, we can gain an intuitive understanding of what a true father should be—and what our heavenly Father actually is. His Word is totally trustworthy. His love and faithfulness are constant. He is the archetypal Father, fulfilling the roles of nourisher, protector, and upholder.

> God is always a true Father to us. He loves us as His own children.

Your deliverance from your pain is in realizing that everything your father lacked is a revelation of what God desires to be in your life. He will be for you what your earthly father couldn't be; He will be the father you never had. Your own father may have abandoned you, but the Scripture assures us, *"When my father and my mother forsake me, then the LORD will take me up"* (Psalm 27:10). You don't have to be angry with your father any longer because your heavenly Father is the redeemer of your earthly father's failure.

God welcomes the weight of parental responsibility. He won't be abrupt or irritated with you. He is patient and kind. He is an understanding mediator. He strengthens and directs. He is both a loving disciplinarian and the giver of blessings. He is the source and illuminator of both natural and spiritual things, teaching you holiness and righteousness. His presence is continually with you, and you can experience a bond of love, trust, and common purpose with Him. God says, *"I will never leave thee, nor forsake thee"* (Hebrews 13:5). He promises to be a *"very present help in trouble"* (Psalm 46:1). He will be close to you in times of distress.

Your own father couldn't supply all your needs, but God the Father anticipates and answers all our needs. The Bible says, *"Your Father knows the things you have need of before you ask Him"* (Matthew 6:8 NKJV), and *"My God shall supply all your need according to his riches in glory by Christ Jesus"* (Philippians 4:19). Whatever you need, ask your heavenly Father for it. *"Ask, and it shall be given you; seek, and ye shall find; knock, and it shall be opened unto you: for every one that asketh receiveth; and he that seeketh findeth; and to him that knocketh it shall be opened"* (Matthew 7:7–8).

The Faithfulness of the Father

One of the reasons that Jesus came to earth was to open our eyes to the fatherhood of God and what that means for us. He taught us many things concerning the faithfulness of our heavenly Father. In one illustration of this truth, He tells the story of a man whose son asked him for bread. In a good father-son relationship, a father would never give his son a stone when he asked for bread. Likewise, he wouldn't give him a snake if he asked for a fish. (See Matthew 7:9–10.) In the same way, when we ask God for help, He will give us what is good and not what is harmful.

There may have been times in your life when your needs should have been met by a parent, but the opposite was given to you—the equivalent of stones and snakes. Our heavenly Father is not like that. If you ask Him to be your Father, He will not disappoint you. He will never withhold from you what is good.

He tells us to ask Him by faith, and He will give us the desires of our hearts. (See Mark 11:24.)

> **God will never withhold from you what is good.**

Jesus said, in effect, "If earthly fathers with an evil nature know how to give good gifts to their children, how much more will your Father who is in heaven give you good things if you ask Him?" (See Matthew 7:11.)

"Father, into Your Hands"

As God's Son, Jesus is our example of how to relate to God as Father. He can show us the path to the healing of our wounds and scars because He is *"touched with the feeling of our infirmities"* (Hebrews 4:15). He understands what it's like to experience the absence of a Father in a time of great need. His relationship with God was so intimate that during His agonizing time on the cross—when He was separated from the Father as He bore our sins—He longed for the sense of His Father's presence. The absence of the constant communion with God that Jesus was accustomed to left Him looking longingly toward heaven, searching for the face of His Father. He cried out, *"My God, my God, why hast thou forsaken me?"* (Matthew 27:46).

Jesus can sympathize with the dark cloud that overshadows your relationship with your father. He knows the tormenting thoughts of despair that congregate just beyond the reach of reason and contribute to your feelings of isolation. He recognizes that your wounds and scars have fastened you to an emotional cross, and that you can be delivered only through the power of God. When you become wounded, you must place your spirit totally into your heavenly Father's hands, as Jesus did, saying, *"Father, into your hands I commit my spirit"* (Luke 23:46 NIV). When you commit yourself to your loving Father, who has the power to renew your spirit, He will heal your emotional wounds and remove the scars of disappointment and lost expectation.

Jesus willingly suffered separation from God while He was on the cross so that you could be restored to fellowship with the Father and never have to be alienated from Him for a moment. God the Father wants to spend time with you—talking to you, loving you, and confirming your relationship with Him. He says, in effect, "I will be there for every trial, every test, and every situation in your life."

> Jesus willingly suffered separation from God so you could be restored to fellowship with the Father.

"This Is My Beloved Son"

The Father also desires to present you to the world as His child, prepared and validated for His purpose, just as He did for Jesus. At the beginning of His ministry, Jesus went to John the Baptist at the Jordan River, where John was baptizing many people as they repented of their sins. John recognized Jesus as the Lamb of God. This recognition gave him a sudden sense of his own unworthiness. His conviction was intensified when Jesus asked to be baptized by him, and he voiced his confusion: *"I need to be baptized by You, and are You coming to me?"* (Matthew 3:14 NKJV). When Jesus convinced John that the request was necessary to fulfill the will of God, he baptized Him.

As Jesus came out of the water, the sky opened, and the Holy Spirit descended on Him in the form of a dove. Then the Father's confirming voice echoed from heaven with pride, *"This is my beloved Son, in whom I am well pleased"* (v. 17). The voice of God approved and validated the Son—presenting Jesus to the people whom He would redeem.

While Jesus was growing up in Nazareth, God the Father had loved and prepared His Son for His life and service on earth. Now, at His baptism, the Father could say, "My Son is ready for His work and is well pleasing in My sight." The confirming voice of the Father was based on the relationship God had shared with Jesus long before His baptism. It speaks of time spent together, instruction given, and strength received.

In John 15:1, we are given a clear illustration of the necessity of our relationship with the Father through the Son. The Father is the gardener, Jesus is the vine, and we are the branches. Through the gardener's clipping, pruning, nourishing, and cherishing, the branches develop maturity and effectiveness—as long as they remain connected to the vine. In other words, the love of the Father through Christ Jesus cultivates, energizes, motivates, and shapes us according to His purpose and plan.

Note that, even though Jesus was spiritually mature when He was baptized, He continually expressed His dependence on His Father. Jesus said, *"The Son can do nothing of himself, but what he seeth the Father do: for what things soever he doeth, these also doeth the Son likewise. For the Father loveth the Son, and showeth him all things that himself doeth"* (John 5:19–20). Likewise, we always need to be dependent on the heavenly Father and do the things that He does. *"Therefore be imitators of God as dear children"* (Ephesians 5:1 NKJV).

It was through the confirmation and empowerment of the Father that Jesus fulfilled God's will. The relationship was so complete that Jesus was certain of His oneness with the Father. He said, *"I and my Father are one"* (John 10:30), and *"He that hath seen me hath seen the Father"* (John 14:9). He was convinced that He was His Father's Son because He had been given the strength, wisdom, and Spirit of the Father. We, also, can experience the Father's validation and empowerment to live the lives that we were created to live. We can do this because we have received the Spirit of the Father. *"The Spirit itself beareth witness with our spirit, that we are the children of God"* (Romans 8:16).

> We can experience the Father's empowerment to live the lives we were created to live.

The Fatherhood of God in the History of His People

In addition to Jesus' teachings on the Father, and the example of His own relationship to God as the Son, we can see examples of the fatherhood of God throughout the Bible. These illustrations show us how God relates to us as Father and how He wants us to respond to Him.

The Father as Source

In Genesis, we learn that God is the originator of all mankind. He creates man and woman and supplies all their physical, emotional, and spiritual needs. We also read about Abraham, whom God promises will become a *"great nation"* (Genesis 12:2) through his descendants. It is this nation's relationship with God that distinguishes it from all other nations. The Father affirms, *"Israel is my son, even my firstborn"* (Exodus 4:22).

The Father as Deliverer

In each phase of Israel's life, God is always present. In Exodus, He hears their cries for help when they are in captivity as Egyptian slaves. As a caring Father, He sends Moses to lead them to freedom. The people are delivered by the living God. Yet, soon afterward, they build a golden calf—reminiscent of the Egyptians' false gods—revealing that, while they are physically free, they are still captive in their hearts. They haven't grasped their true identity as God's children or the relationship that God desires to have with them. They haven't given their heavenly Father the honor and love that He deserves. As a loving disciplinarian, God chastises them, yet ultimately blesses them as His people.

The Father as Teacher

In Leviticus, God gives the children of Israel rules of conduct to instruct them in the way of holiness. He teaches them moral, ethical, and religious behavior, but also shows them how to have a relationship with Him through sacrifice and worship.

The Father as Shepherd

In Numbers, we see that the Father stays with His people even in their disobedience and lack of faith, and sustains them through forty years of wandering in the desert of Sinai. This wilderness experience becomes God's tutorial for them—a bridge from bondage to blessing. The Father tends His flock as He guides them through the wilderness.

The Father as Promise-Keeper

In Deuteronomy, we again find a description of the Israelites' disobedience and lack of faith, as well as God's instructions on how they are to live and serve Him. I think that the Father repeats these instructions in His Word because He wants His children (ourselves included) to understand His intentions. One of the lessons of this book is that we must learn how to trust God and fight in the Spirit in order to reach the place that He has promised. As it says in Romans, we must be *"fully persuaded that, what he* [has] *promised, he* [is] *able also to perform"* (4:21).

The Father as Defender

In the book of Joshua, the Israelites finally enter into the Promised Land. God the Father teaches them a new lesson of His love and power in an effort to equip them for the next phase of their journey: Obedience and praise will pull down the walls of any adversary. Although the Israelites are equipped for further success, they forfeit it because they are again unfaithful and turn away from their God.

> Obedience and praise will pull down the walls of any adversary.

The Father as Loving Disciplinarian

In Judges, we see that a loving Father's mercy always exceeds His disappointment. He prunes the vine, cutting it back but leaving enough to bear fruit again.

The Father as Kinsman-Redeemer

The book of Ruth shows that there is deliverance for those who will cling to God as Father, despite the hardships and temptations of the world. Ruth the Moabitess speaks beautiful words of commitment when she tells her mother-in-law, Naomi, after the death of their husbands, *"Entreat me not to leave thee, or to return from following after thee: for whither thou goest, I will go; and where thou lodgest, I will lodge: thy people shall be my people, and thy God my God"* (Ruth 1:16). The Father prepares a harvest field and a kinsman-redeemer, Boaz, to bless the faithfulness of one who so easily could have returned to a people who did not acknowledge Him. Boaz tells Ruth, *"A full reward be given thee of the LORD God of Israel, under whose wings thou art come to trust"* (2:12).

The Father as Faithful One

Through 1 and 2 Samuel, 1 and 2 Kings, and 1 and 2 Chronicles, God shows His loving patience with an imperfect people whose continual wrong choices never discourage His faithfulness to them. The Lord demonstrates that He will never leave or forsake His children. Making His will clear, He blesses obedience and chastises those who disobey Him. Through it all, His desire is to reveal His glory to the world.

The Father as Restorer

A disciplining Father allows the Israelites to be taken into captivity by the Babylonians following their disobedience and rebellion against Him. Yet, in Ezra and Nehemiah, He gently restores a remnant of His people to their land and defeats those who oppose their plans to rebuild the walls and temple of Jerusalem. He also reminds them of His law so that they will learn to love and follow Him.

The Father as Grace-Giver

In Esther, God again shows His lovingkindness and power to deliver the Israelites when they face adverse conditions. In their distress, His people humble themselves in prayer and fasting. They receive God's grace and defeat their enemies in a demonstration of the Father's faithfulness to His people.

The Father as Lord of One and All

In Job, Psalms, Proverbs, Ecclesiastes, and Song of Solomon, God confirms that He is the Lord of all—but also the Father of each individual. He tests His people because He knows that what He has purposed for them will ultimately stand in the face of trial. He is aware of their defeats as well as their victories, yet He welcomes them into His presence. He provides safety when they walk in the valley of the shadow of death, and shelter under the shadow of His wings. His Word provides wisdom for His children. He instructs and warns them about the vain elements of life. The Father sings a prophetic love song to His people, a message about the unity of Christ and the church. He demonstrates that He is a God of relationship—protecting, caring for, and loving those who belong to Him.

> God is the Lord of all—but also the Father of each individual.

The Father as Sovereign Lord

The books of the major prophets—Isaiah, Jeremiah, Lamentations, Ezekiel, and Daniel—speak of a Father who saves, appoints, strengthens, and warns us while sovereignly controlling all things. Through the words of His prophets, He gives us a glimpse of the future while keeping us focused on our present need to maintain our relationships with Him.

The Father as Sustainer

The ensemble of minor prophets—Hosea, Joel, Amos, Obadiah, Jonah, Micah, Nahum, Habakkuk, Zephaniah, Haggai, Zechariah, and Malachi—confirms God's saving power. We see that He is a faithful and loving heavenly Father who sustains and blesses His children. We also encounter an amazing truth: God Himself must visit the earth in order to fully redeem mankind from rebellion and sin.

The Father as Redeemer

In the New Testament, Emmanuel (meaning "God with us") is sent from the Father to be born into the world. Jesus teaches us about the fatherhood of God and the nature of His kingdom. He dies to redeem us from our sins, rises again, and returns to the Father to reign in heaven. Jesus' sacrifice breaks the barrier between Jews and Gentiles so that not only Israel, but also all the people of the earth who believe in Him, can call God their Father.

> *You are a chosen generation, a royal priesthood, a holy nation, His own special people, that you may proclaim the praises of Him who called you out of darkness into His marvelous light; who once were not a people but are now the people of God, who had not obtained mercy but now have obtained mercy.* (1 Peter 2:9–10 NKJV)

Through Jesus, our relationship with God becomes more personal than ever as we receive the gift of the Father—*His very Spirit to live within us.* Through His Spirit, we can reflect His nature and character and become His true sons and daughters.

The history of God's relationship with His people in both the Old and New Testaments reveals that God has always been humanity's Father. Even though mankind has continually turned away from Him, He has provided a way for us to be restored to Him and to receive all the benefits, responsibilities, and blessings of being His children.

The Ideal Father

Being healed of our wounds and scars often comes down to a matter of trust in the fatherhood of God. Trust enables us to recognize that He is with us in the midst of the fires of life. Trust gives us hope in His purposes for our lives. It gives us courage to enter into the Father's presence, drop our masks, and reveal our true hearts to Him. *"There is no fear in love; but perfect love casteth out fear: because fear hath torment. He that feareth is not made perfect in love. We love him, because he first loved us"* (1 John 4:18–19). We trust God when we understand that He is a faithful Parent whose love delivers us from life's woundings and makes us whole.

No matter what kind of relationship you had with your earthly father, you can know that your heavenly Father loves you and will always be present with you. He seeks to heal you and to fill the void in your heart with His light and life. He is your faithful God and Father.

> Your heavenly Father loves you and will always be present with you.

In the next chapter, we will see how living continually in the presence of our heavenly Father and not letting anything interfere with that relationship enables us to come through the fires of life without scars.

Spiritual Fathers and Children

Before I close this chapter, I would like to add a word about spiritual fathers and children because a misunderstanding of the nature of this relationship can also cause much wounding and scarring. Just as we need our natural fathers' love and guidance, we require spiritual fathers who can show us God's love, guide us into spiritual maturity, and help us to discover and implement His purposes for our lives. While some people's parents may fulfill both roles to some extent, we often have a need for mentorship from another mature Christian (or Christians).

The apostle Paul revealed the special role of spiritual fatherhood in 1 Corinthians 4:15 when he wrote, *"Though you might have ten thousand instructors in Christ, yet you do not have many fathers"* (NKJV). Spiritual fathers are those who birth others into ministry. They help empower people to fulfill their spiritual destinies by loving, covering, motivating, cultivating, pruning, correcting, and passing on their strengths to them.

> We need spiritual fathers to help us implement God's purposes in our lives.

Not All Pastors Are Spiritual Fathers

Spiritual fathering requires a desire to instruct and develop people in their ministries or callings. It is more than sowing truth into people's lives; it includes spending time with them, imparting spiritual wisdom and strength, and providing guidance. Spiritual fathers are gifted by the power of the Holy Spirit but don't necessarily hold specific leadership positions in the church. Those who do not understand this reality often experience disappointment and discouragement in their desire for a mentor.

Many people have a silent expectation that all pastors are spiritual fathers. Consequently, they expect their pastors to help them to develop their personal ministries. Their assumption is based on the pastors' position and doesn't take into consideration whether or not they are gifted for mentoring.

The list of spiritual gifts in Ephesians 4:11 includes apostles, prophets, evangelists, pastors, and teachers. A pastor does not necessarily have dual gifts of pastoring and apostleship. A shepherd tends, leads, guides, feeds, and directs, but is not the father of the sheep. There is an element of fathering in shepherding, but fathering is distinct in its approach and purpose.

It is very common, however, for a person to develop a sense of fatherly expectation of a pastor. This expectation is based on the belief that just being associated with and working closely with the pastor will produce a father-child relationship. Many times, this person seeks to have the same anointing as the pastor. When this doesn't happen, he or she may start to distrust the pastoral relationship and the validity of spiritual mentoring.

What adds to the confusion is that many pastors believe that they *should* be spiritual fathers because they either are taught or assume that this is one of their roles. Again, if they are not gifted in this area, they will be ineffective in it. Eventually, the supposed sons and daughters will become resentful, thinking that the leader is withholding what they need. They may even draw the false conclusion that either jealousy or insecurity on the part of the pastor is to blame when the real reason is a lack of gifting. In these situations, people may become disillusioned by the time the leader realizes that he has no gifting or interest in fathering.

Another dimension to this problem is that many people believe it is the pastor's role to supply what has been lacking in their lives. If they did not have strong parental relationships, they expect their pastors to fill that particular void. In this way, they approach their leaders with an emotional agenda that the leaders are often unaware of. When their expectations are unfulfilled, they may become resentful. The feelings of betrayal and distrust that took root in their previous relationships grow deeper. Now they feel rejected not only by those who disappointed them in the past, but also by their current pastors. These feelings can be so intense that they may begin to speak negatively about their churches without anyone ever knowing the real reason.

These wounded people usually begin a heartbreaking journey in which they go from ministry to ministry with an unspoken need while their bitterness continues to build. Driven by negative emotions, they come to feel that God and the church don't care about them, while in reality the problem lies in their unarticulated needs and expectations.

> The father-child relationship requires commitment to being mentored.

Instead of automatically assuming that our pastors can fulfill our need for a spiritual father, we should ask our heavenly Father to bring the right mentors into our lives. He can connect us to the spiritual fathers who can help us to mature and become all that He has created us to be.

A Commitment to Being Spiritually Fathered

How does the process of spiritual fathering occur? Again, mere proximity to a person or being taught by that person will not produce a father-child relationship. It takes a commitment to being mentored and receiving what the father has to impart.

In Luke 15, Jesus taught the parable of the prodigal son. The father in this story has two sons. Both grew up in the same house, but the older son lives in obedience to his father while the younger son does not. The younger son has benefited from the father's care and gifts. However, he is not in a submissive relationship with his father and does not appear to honor him. This younger, immature child feels restricted by the structure of the father's house. He desires to do his own thing long before he is ready to function on his own.

This son may have cooperated with his father at times, but cooperation is not necessarily the same thing as submission. We can agree to do something even though our attitude about it is poor. We cooperate, but inside, we're resisting. It is not unreasonable to assume that the son obeyed with a heart that was not fully submitted. Sometimes we need to accept and do what we don't want to do based on our trust in the father's experience and the honor that we have for him.

How many times has a leader sensed a follower's insincere obedience? Remember that God accepted Abel's sacrifice and rejected Cain's because of the attitudes of their hearts. (See Genesis 4:1-7.) An unsubmitted heart often leads to resentment and rebellion. As these fester, they can produce strong emotions of independence and can cause sons and daughters to want to separate from their fathers. When this happens, it is very common for the sons and daughters to believe that God is telling them to move on to another church or mentor. However, this is not inspiration, but rather a self-fulfilling prophecy—a word created by our own emotions that facilitates our own desires while energizing our self-will.

In the parable, the younger son approaches the father and asks for his inheritance, which the father reluctantly gives him. The son then heads off to try to duplicate his father's domain, and the results are tragic. He fails miserably because he has some of his father's gifts but none of his father's wisdom or experience. Likewise, God may give an anointing for ministry to a person, but the correct application of this anointing comes through time, wisdom, and the right circumstances. When spiritual children prematurely believe that they have been inspired to go out on their own, they seek to pull away from the very fathers they need to learn from in order to fulfill their callings. Their problem is their heart attitudes and their misunderstanding of the importance of God's timing.

Many people pull away from their spiritual fathers during the critical season of development and maturation when their gifts are present but "raw." During this season, the fathers' instruction and guidance seem restrictive and God seems to be taking His time in promoting them to their own ministries. Impatience sets in, and the offspring, who are still tender shoots, uproot themselves.

I have noticed that during this season of development, men have a tendency to approach their spiritual fathers in a competitive way. They try to impress them rather than to receive from their children. Spiritual fathers must understand this natural tendency and continually exercise grace and wisdom in dealing with them. They must patiently refine the positive qualities while pruning the negative ones so that a true son may be developed.

People often react like sheep when they need to be corrected. When a shepherd has to administer medicine to a sheep, the sheep's reaction is to flee from the presence of the shepherd, getting as far away as he possibly can. He distances himself within the flock or attempts to leave the pasture. It is not until the sheep has wandered away that he realizes that the shepherd's administration was beneficial.

The same thing happens in the spiritual father-child relationship. The realization of the need for the father often comes in the midst of negative circumstances that prove that the son or daughter was not as mature or gifted as he or she once thought. Sometimes pride delays a return to the father. Yet once pride loses the fight, the son or daughter usually comes "home."

The loving father in Luke 15 receives and restores the Prodigal Son when the son realizes his error and returns. The same should occur in a spiritual fathering relationship except, perhaps, if the child has actively tried to destroy the reputation and work of the father. This may make it difficult for them to return to the same relationship that they used to have.

Hindrances to Effective Spiritual Parenting

Insecurity

Sometimes, problems in spiritual mentoring originate with the father. Often, the gift of fatherhood is rendered powerless when the mentor is insecure. This is because insecure leaders are often very hesitant to share their strengths. Their hesitancy creates a very stifling environment for the sons and daughters. It is not uncommon for these leaders to create a negative relationship or circumstance that discourages those who follow, instead of cultivating their strengths. As a result, strong, gifted sons and daughters may become disheartened and remain untrained in their callings. When this occurs, the ministry at large can suffer.

One of the telltale signs of insecurity is when a leader does not have consistent ministry help. Spiritual fathers have a tendency to attract sons and daughters to assist them in their work. However, there are times when the leader is distancing himself from others not because he is insecure, but simply because he has been hurt by followers in the past.

Hurt Feelings

It is not uncommon for a leader to extend himself by sowing into the life of another and nurturing that person's spiritual growth, only to watch the person become "strong" and decide that he doesn't need the leader any longer. We talked about this tendency in an earlier section, but let's consider it now from the father's perspective. When this type of behavior occurs, a leader can become hesitant about participating in mentoring. This hesitancy may even start to bleed over into his other relationships. He may develop a general distrust of others and come to believe that spiritual fathering is a waste of time, resources, and effort.

> Healthy spiritual mentoring comes down to love, faithfulness, commitment, and trust.

It can be extremely discouraging to mentor someone who has no spiritual direction, and to assist that person in understanding his purpose, only to hear him say that he no longer respects your leadership or instruction. The father perceives this reaction as disloyalty—and the disloyalty of one's followers can be a source of much pain for leaders.

Healthy Spiritual Mentoring

Spiritual fathers should seek to reflect the love and truth of the heavenly father, while spiritual children should show love and respect for their mentors. Yet relationships between spiritual fathers and children are just as prone to lost expectations, disappointment, and hurt as natural family relationships. When these things occur, we should deal with the effects in the same way we would with our families—with understanding and forgiveness, and by putting our ultimate trust in our heavenly Father, the *"father of our spirits"* (Hebrews 12:9 NIV), who never leaves or forsakes us.

Let me conclude by saying that spiritual parenting relationships should not be entered into lightly. The son or daughter should know the character and reputation of the leader, and the leader should know the attitudes and motivations of the son or daughter. Expectations and assumptions should be discussed. There must be a commitment to one another's spiritual and emotional health and well-being. The son or daughter has to be able to trust the leader's wisdom and spiritual maturity, and the father must be able to trust the faithfulness and respect of the son or daughter. As in healthy parent-child relationships, healthy spiritual mentoring comes down to these things: love, communication, commitment, faithfulness, and trust.

Chapter Six

The Power of the Presence

"In him we live, and move, and have our being."
—Acts 17:28

After we come to understand that God is our Father, we also must recognize that we can have joy, strength, and freedom when we maintain a personal relationship with Him. We can continually draw on His loving and powerful presence to meet all our needs as we look to Him for healing and deliverance from our emotional pain. His presence will also keep us connected to His grace as we face future challenges so that we can go through them without becoming scarred. Jacob learned this truth—the hard way.

Recognizing His Presence

As far back as Jacob can remember, he has been self-serving and agenda-driven. His brief periods of guilt for his actions are never enough to ignite a spark of change. He is always sorry—but not for very long.

Jacob never seems able to please his father, Isaac. The friendship that should have existed between them is somehow always out of reach. The things that he is good at don't interest Isaac. Jacob always feels that he never quite measures up. His older brother, Esau, however, appears to do no wrong in his father's eyes. Envious of the close relationship between his father and brother, Jacob gravitates to his mother, Rebekah, who has always favored her younger son.

Though Jacob has found a friend in his mother, their relationship has cultivated his natural tendency toward manipulation. Instead of correcting his agenda, she has excused it—even encouraged it. In this household, a sense of impending family breakdown is always in the air. Sooner or later, the whole situation is bound to erupt, and it does—the day that Jacob maneuvers to obtain Esau's blessing. This blessing technically belongs to Esau as the firstborn, although the Lord previously told Rebekah, *"The elder shall serve the younger"* (Genesis 25:23).

A desire for wealth and power can bring out the worst in people, and it does so in Jacob. His father has enough riches to provide well for both his sons, but the exclusive honor is given to the oldest. Jacob had already bargained with Esau and obtained his birthright. (See Genesis 25:29–34.) Now he also seeks the blessing—the blessing of those who are Abraham's descendants. Rebekah convinces Jacob that this honor should be his, and they deceive Isaac so that he gives Esau's blessing to Jacob. (Although the Lord intended Jacob to have this blessing, Jacob and Rebekah are trying to fulfill the promise in their own strength instead of trusting God to work things out in His own time.) When Esau finds out, he vows to kill his brother. Following Rebekah's advice, Jacob leaves his family behind and flees to his Uncle Laban's house in another land.

Jacob's fundamental problem is not his manipulation—that is just a symptom. His wounds and scars come from not having a true relationship with the Lord. He could have trusted God to fulfill his purpose in life instead of resorting to deception and fraud.

Even though the household that Jacob grew up in was dysfunctional, it was also God-centered. Jacob had heard his father's stories of how the Lord had helped the family in the past. His grandfather, Abraham, was honored and revered. He trusted God and was preserved through many trials and tests. Jacob heard stories of how God had miraculously provided for the family during times of famine and in the face of their enemies. His

> Jacob's perception of God was limited by his lack of relationship with Him.

own father's birth was miraculously provided for by God, since he had been born when his parents were in their old age. But these things reflected his grandfather's and his father's relationships with God—not his.

Jacob felt that God was not involved in his own circumstances. Though he'd heard his father talk about God, he never really gained an understanding of Him. His mother's desire to overlook his shortcomings instead of correcting them didn't help his spiritual growth. Though he is aware of God, Jacob's perception of Him is limited by his lack of relationship with Him.

Jacob doesn't seem to become aware of God's immediate presence in his life until he is on his way to his Uncle Laban's house and has a dream.

So he came to a certain place and stayed there all night, because the sun had set. And he took one of the stones of that place and put it at his head, and he lay down in that place to sleep. Then he dreamed, and behold, a ladder was set up on the earth, and its top reached to heaven; and there the angels of God were ascending and descending on it. And behold, the LORD stood above it and said: "I am the LORD God of Abraham your father and the God of Isaac; the land on which you lie I will give to you and your descendants. Also your descendants shall be as the dust of the earth; you shall spread abroad to the west and the east, to the north and the south; and in you and in your seed all the families of the earth shall be blessed. Behold, I am with you and will keep you wherever you go, and will bring you back to this land; for I will not leave you until I have done what I have spoken to you." (Genesis 28:11–15 NKJV)

When Jacob awakes, he has a sudden awareness of the presence and power of God, and says, *"Surely the LORD is in this place, and I did not know it"* (v. 16 NKJV). In other words, he recognizes that the I AM is present with him. He calls the place Bethel, which means "house of God." Jacob was in the presence of his Help, but he hadn't realized it. In a sense, he believed that his problem and his geographic location excluded the presence of God. As soon as he realizes that God is with him, he understands that the Lord is available to help him in his personal situation.

God Is Always with Us

No matter where we find ourselves or how personal our problems are, God is willing and able to help us. Jacob had the promise of God, but he hadn't fully understood the power of His presence. It was not until he recognized the presence that the promises were made available to him. Likewise, once we understand that God is our heavenly Father, it is important for us to truly recognize His immediate presence in our lives. When we don't maintain our relationships with Him, this keeps us from walking in, receiving, and releasing His promises. Let's look at several things that can block us from remaining in His presence.

Misconceptions That Hinder Our Experience of His Presence

God Is Powerful, but Not Loving

First, the way you view God will either limit or release His power in your life. It is possible to know God without being fully aware of all that He is and all that He wants to do for you. His only real "limitation" is our limited perception of Him. We can't exercise faith for our life situations based on all that He has to offer us if perception is limited. He is much greater than we think He is.

> God is much greater than we think He is.

For example, we can have a sense of God's power, but not His love. If we think of God only as Creator and Judge, we may never perceive Him as the healer of our souls. Creation and its results are evidences of His power. However, that evidence doesn't totally define Him or reveal all that He is able to do. Likewise, a God of power, lightening, smoke, and earthquakes (see Exodus 19:16–18) can seem impersonal and distant if we don't also know that He is a gentle Shepherd (see Isaiah 40:11). Knowing Him in all His facets helps us to draw close to Him for the healing of our hurts.

God Is Present Only in Certain "Holy" Places

We often don't truly understand that God is present with us *right now*. Theoretically, we know that God is present everywhere, but we don't act as if this is true. Again, we relate to Him as if He is remote, untouchable, and impersonal, and we pray as if He is far away. We plead for God to come to us, as if He is at a distance.

We sometimes talk about God as if He is not present at the time. We imagine that He is located only in certain "holy" places, such as a church. There are certain things we will say in other places that we will not say in church because we subconsciously think God isn't listening. These beliefs limit our perception of and access to Him.

Like Jacob, we can find ourselves in the presence of God without perceiving Him. When Jacob went to sleep on the ground that night, he didn't associate the place with God, so he was unaware that God was available to help him there. Likewise, we think that God must be "ushered into" our presence when He is already here. *"For he hath said, I will never leave thee, nor forsake thee. So that we may boldly say, The Lord is my helper, and I will not fear what man shall do unto me"* (Hebrews 13:5–6).

> Wherever you are, God is. You are never alone.

Perhaps your promise hasn't been released because you're still thinking that God is "out there" somewhere. If you have believed in and received Christ, then you have God's Holy Spirit dwelling within you. If the Spirit of God dwells in you, then God's presence lives in you, because *"God is a Spirit"* (John 4:24). The promises are present because God is present.

Wherever you are, God is. You are never alone. Even if you are the only believer on your job, in your neighborhood, or in your household, you are in His presence right now. Once you truly understand this truth and live in the confidence of it, your prayers are going to change, and you are going to change.

God Responds to "Religiosity"

Religious traditions, ceremonies, and rituals of all types have done much to hinder our perception of God's presence because they have become mechanical replacements for true relationship. Even styles of worship and praise can become symbols and substitutes for closeness with God. Likewise, prayer was given to us for communication with God, but when it is ritualized, it can distance us from Him rather than bringing us closer to Him.

We are not meant to have fellowship with God by our own techniques and power, but by the Spirit of God. (See Zechariah 4:6.) When we are taught to *"pray without ceasing"* (1 Thessalonians 5:17), I don't think this means that we are supposed to verbalize our prayers twenty-four hours a day—although we are meant to talk with God frequently. I think it means that we are to have a constant consciousness of His presence so that we are continually drawing on His strength, love, and wisdom. When a couple walks down the street holding hands, they may not be saying anything to one another, but they are aware of each other's presence. Likewise, when we know that God is present with us, He doesn't have to say something to us all the time, and we don't have to constantly say something to Him, to be aware of each other's presence and to share loving fellowship.

Looking to Others rather than to God

We can lose a sense of God's ever present help by looking to other people for solutions to our problems when they are unable to give us what we need. This is not to say that we

> When you experience pain and rejection, first call on your heavenly Father.

shouldn't sometimes seek the prayers and wisdom of spiritual leaders and mature Christians when we are struggling with emotional issues. However, when you experience pain and rejection—or any storm of life—first call on your heavenly Father's help. *"For as many as are led by the Spirit of God, they are the sons of God"* (Romans 8:14).

Feeling Afraid or Guilty before God

We can undermine our relationships with God when we succumb to feelings of fear and guilt and "run away" from Him because we're not sure how He will react to us. Sometimes, we are afraid of our loved one's reactions to something that occurred in our pasts or something that we have done. It's not our loved ones' integrity we worry about; we're concerned about whether they will continue to love us after they know who we *really* are. Some people live every day under the specter of fearful thoughts, such as "Is this going to be the day when he or she will discover the truth about me and reject me?"

People often react in the same way with God. Yet the Scripture assures us,

> For we have not an high priest which cannot be touched with the feeling of our infirmities; but was in all points tempted like as we are, yet without sin. Let us therefore come boldly unto the throne of grace, that we may obtain mercy, and find grace to help in time of need. (Hebrews 4:15–16)

Jesus said, *"Come unto me, all ye that labour and are heavy laden, and I will give you rest"* (Matthew 11:28). The Father is saying to us, in effect, "Even though you have made mistakes or failed, come to Me. Even though you can't look Me in the face, I still want you. I desire to forgive and restore you." *"For ye have not received the spirit of bondage again to fear; but ye have received the Spirit of adoption, whereby we cry, Abba, Father"* (Romans 8:15).

Blaming God

When our lives have been wounded and scarred by an absence of good relationships and a lack of support from the significant people in our lives, we may blame God for our troubles. We may also be angry at either the poor choices we have made or the hurtful actions others have committed against us—and we then direct our anger toward God. This often happens when the offending person is out of reach or is insensitive to our pain, or when we have difficulty accepting our own poor choices. God is a convenient target for our hurt and frustration, especially because He doesn't appear to defend Himself against our charges, but instead seems silent.

> You have to allow God to be the Father that He wants to be for you.

If you've been wounded by someone else, don't react by keeping God at a distance. Rejection can shut you down to the things of God, as we saw in Michal's life in the previous chapter. You have to allow God to be the Father that He wants to be for you. Release your anger, and run to Him. Again, don't be angry with others if they weren't equipped to give you what you needed. Instead, forgive them and pray to God, "Heavenly Father, set me free from these feelings of rejection so that I may praise and love You. I'm so wounded that I don't trust love. I don't know how to give or receive it. Be for me what others were unable to be. Heal me of my wounds and scars. Help me to know that I am Your child and that You will never leave or forsake me."

Thinking We Can Do without God's Help

In the parable of the prodigal son, the younger son thought that he could handle his life without his father's direction, so he took his inheritance and left his father's home. At first, he seemed to be living well, but circumstances soon turned against him. He ended up working as a keeper of pigs with barely enough food to sustain himself.

Need has a tendency to produce insight. The Prodigal Son began to contemplate his situation and what life could be if he returned to his father's house, even as a servant. The Bible uses the phrase *"he came to himself"* (Luke 15:17). This means that he analyzed his life based on its potential, looked at his present circumstances, and realized that he needed his father after all. He came to understand how critical his relationship with his father was, and he sought to reestablish contact with him.

His perception of both himself and his father were radically changed. He began to rehearse what he needed to say to enter into his father's graces once more. The son who had rejected his father was looking for a way to enter his presence so he could hear his father's voice again. He was convicted, and he was contrite. The last time he had spoken to his father, he had made a declaration based on his supposed manhood. I think that, this time, the cry of his heart was for his "Abba." It was a cry of intense need for the father's love and strength. The son realized that the father had the ability to supply all his needs. The son was old enough to know his own inability compared to the capabilities of his father, and he knew that his father was the only one who could help him. The fruit of failure is often bitter, but it can be extremely beneficial if we learn from it.

We frequently act like the Prodigal Son in our relationships with our heavenly Father. We may begin to spend less time fellowshipping with Him in worship and prayer and reading His Word because we forget how much we need Him to sustain our lives. Then, circumstances or relationships don't work out for us, and we run out of our own strength and ability to cope.

I've found that wisdom is often birthed in the worst of times. When we find ourselves in troublesome situations, we begin to remember the life-sustaining advice, direction, and correction we have received from God at other times. We "come to ourselves," and this drives us to return to God's original intention for us, which is continual communion with Him.

> You may run away from God, but He will never turn away from you.

When we are honest about our failures, all our excuses are removed from the equation. We take a long look at our own reflection and understand that there is little room for placing blame on others. Yet our pain propels us to seek a close relationship with our heavenly Father again. His presence and Word, which we formerly ignored, become the catalyst of our restoration.

When the Prodigal Son came to himself, he said, *"I will arise and go to my father"* (Luke 15:18). He knew his father's character, and he never had any doubt that he could go to him for help. Though he thinks he will return as a servant, he is greeted as a son. What a wonderful truth this is. When we have a relationship with God, He says, *"I will never leave thee, nor forsake thee"* (Hebrews 13:5). This means that you may run away from Him, but He will never turn away from you. *"If we are faithless, He remains faithful; He cannot deny Himself"* (2 Timothy 2:13 NKJV). You can always return to Him because He never stops being your Father.

God Has Always Made His Presence Known

God has always sought ways to reveal Himself to us. He wants us to know Him *truly* and *personally*. From His visits with Adam in the garden in the cool of the day (see Genesis 3:8), to His instructions for creating a Tent of Meeting, which was His appointed meeting place with the Israelites (see Exodus 29:42–46 NIV), to His sending of Jesus, who is *"Emmanuel,…God with us"* (Matthew 1:23), our heavenly Father has always shown that He desires to dwell among His people and have a close relationship with them.

> God is Shepherd as well as Judge, Healer as well as Creator.

> *From one man he made every nation of men, that they should inhabit the whole earth; and he determined the times set for them and the exact places where they should live. God did this so that men would seek him and perhaps reach out for him and find him, though **he is not far from each one of us**. "For in him we live and move and have our being."* (Acts 17:26–28 NIV, emphasis added)

Our relationship with the Father is the basis on which we can come to Him for healing. He requires only that we believe He is everything that He says He is—that He is Shepherd as well as Judge, Healer as well as Creator. God is all-powerful, all-knowing, and all-loving. He is unhindered by the restrictions of time or space; He is unfazed when presented with little or nothing to work with. He is wherever you are, and He has the power to meet all your needs.

> *Whither shall I go from thy spirit? or whither shall I flee from thy presence? If I ascend up into heaven, thou art there: if I make my bed in hell, behold, thou art there. If I take the wings of the morning, and dwell in the uttermost parts of the sea; even there shall thy hand lead me, and thy right hand shall hold me. If I say, Surely the darkness shall cover me; even the night shall be light about me. Yea, the darkness hideth not from thee; but the night shineth as the day: the darkness and the light are both alike to thee.*
> (Psalm 139:7–12)

In God's Presence Is Provision

We can be assured that God's help is very present when we need it. *"God is our refuge and strength, a very present help in trouble"* (Psalm 46:1). There is not only a nearness, but also a provision, to God's presence. I believe that, if I am insufficient in something, I just have not yet understood who He is in regard to that area of need in my life. It is impossible to dwell in God's presence and remain empty, incomplete, or fractured. *"My grace is sufficient for thee: for my strength is made perfect in weakness"* (2 Corinthians 12:9).

In the presence of God, all our needs are met. Since God created everything and owns everything, then there's nothing He can't provide for us. If we abide in Him, as Jesus abided in the Father, we will pray in accordance with His will and receive provision for all our needs. The key is remaining in His presence. Jesus said, *"If ye abide in me, and my words abide in you, ye shall ask what ye will, and it shall be done unto you"* (John 15:7).

The Recreating and Restoring Presence

The Father is not just the Creator and Restorer of *things*. He is the Creator and Restorer of *people*. The wounds and scars that life has inflicted are well within His power to heal. He creates new hearts and restores lost hopes. He resurrects our expectations for life.

God is aware that you have been wounded and are in need of healing. He has been touched by the feeling of your infirmities through the unity He has with His Son, Jesus Christ. Love, mercy, grace, and compassion are the tools that God uses as He sews up the wounds of the past. He wants to heal your broken heart and bring peace to the troubled places in your emotions while delivering you from destructive and non-productive behaviors. The Bible tells us, *"The LORD is close to the brokenhearted and saves those who are crushed in spirit"* (Psalm 34:18 NIV), and *"He heals the brokenhearted and binds up their wounds"* (Psalm 147:3 NIV).

God creates new hearts and restores lost hopes.

The Sustaining and Transforming Presence

The Father is always alert to our needs. *"He that keepeth Israel shall neither slumber nor sleep"* (Psalm 121:4). The enemy may try to distract us from His presence by bringing us trouble, but this doesn't mean that God has gone away. He's still there with us.

It was God's presence that sustained Joseph during all his trials of rejection, slavery, false accusation, and imprisonment.

The Bible tells us, *"The LORD was with Joseph"* (Genesis 39:2, 21). Because the Lord was with him every step of the way, Joseph was healed of his wounds of betrayal, disappointment, and isolation so that he could forgive his brothers and fulfill his destiny of preserving his family for the purposes of God.

The presence of the Lord enabled Moses to confront Pharaoh, lead the Israelites out of Egypt, and guide God's people in the desert. The Israelites followed God in the wilderness through the cloud by day and the fire by night. (See Exodus 13:21.) Everyone saw the cloud and the fire, but *"the LORD spoke to Moses face to face, as a man speaks to his friend"* (Exodus 33:11 NKJV).

The Lord had a close relationship with Moses, and He wants the same with us. He told Moses, *"My presence shall go with thee"* (v. 14). When God revealed Himself to Moses on the mountain, Moses' face was transformed. *"[Moses] was not aware that his face was radiant because he had spoken with the LORD"* (Exodus 34:29 NIV). What was true for Moses can be true for us: The presence of God is a transforming power.

> The presence of God is a transforming power.

It was God's presence that enabled David to *"fear no evil"* in the *"valley of the shadow of death"* (Psalm 23:4) for, as David said, *"Thou art with me"* (v. 4). Jesus expressed the importance of the presence of God in His life: *"He that sent me is with me: the Father hath not left me alone; for I do always those things that please him"* (John 8:29); *"I am not alone, because the Father is with me"* (John 16:32). It was God's presence that sustained Joseph, Moses, David, and our Savior. The same will be true for us as we maintain our relationship with Him.

The God of Personal Relationships

We must experience a shift in our perceptions concerning God if we are to live continually in His presence. Again, we have to comprehend that He is not unreachable or untouchable. The God of personal relationships is concerned about you. He loves you so much that He makes Himself available to you by faith—faith in who He is and what He is able to do. Once your perception of God broadens to include not only Creator and Judge, but also Restorer and Healer, you will have a renewed personal relationship with Him and be able to reach out to Him for healing.

> *For thus says the high and exalted One who lives forever, whose name is Holy, "I dwell on a high and holy place, and also with the contrite and lowly of spirit in order to revive the spirit of the lowly and to revive the heart of the contrite. For I will not contend forever, neither will I always be angry; for the spirit would grow faint before Me, and the breath of those whom I have made....I have seen his ways, but I will heal him; I will lead him and restore comfort to him and to his mourners, creating the praise of the lips. Peace, peace to him who is far and to him who is near," says the LORD, "and I will heal him."* (Isaiah 57:15–16, 18–19 NASB)

If there is pain and confusion in your life, God's presence will restore peace and order. *"Seek ye first the [presence of the] kingdom of God, and his righteousness; and all these things shall be added unto you"* (Matthew 6:33). God's original intent for your life is a full relationship with Him, which includes His love, compassion, wisdom, and an inheritance He has prepared for you. Whatever has kept you away from God is preventing you from receiving all the Father has for you as His child.

Whatever your internal issues, no matter who was at fault in creating your troubles, God is a loving Father who is ready to receive, love, and heal you.

The Father Is Waiting to Welcome You

Jesus said, *"Surely I am with you always, to the very end of the age"* (Matthew 28:20 NIV). Like the father of the Prodigal Son, God has been looking and waiting for you to come to Him. He desires to embrace you and shower you with compassion. Note that the Prodigal's father—who Jesus told us is a picture of our heavenly Father—never chastised, punished, or rejected the son when he returned. When the son confessed, *"Father, I have sinned against heaven, and in thy sight, and am no more worthy to be called thy son"* (Luke 15:21), the father forgave him, loved him, received him back into the family, and immediately began to restore him to his previous status. He called his servants to begin the process of restoration by putting a robe on him, placing a ring on his finger, and putting shoes on his feet. The unfaithful son experienced the faithfulness of the father.

> The unfaithful son experienced the faithfulness of the father.

I believe that the servants represent the Holy Spirit. The robe, ring, and shoes refer to our identity and position as God's children, and our restored authority in Him. *"What then shall we say to these things? If* [the Father] *is for us, who can be against us?"* (Romans 8:31 NKJV).

Our faithful Father will freely give us everything we need to help us become all that He desires us to be. He could lay charges against us, but instead, He declares us righteous. He could condemn us, but instead, He intercedes for us. Nothing can separate us from the love of our good and faithful Father. (See Romans 8:33–35.)

The Prodigal Son was tired, dirty, ragged, and probably smelled like the hogs he used to tend. Yet, when his father saw him coming, he didn't say, "I told you so," or ask where the money had gone. The father had everything his son needed. He ran and kissed him on the neck and restored a full life to him. He said, *"My son was dead, and is alive again; he was lost, and is found"* (Luke 15:24). The father got his son back, and the son was restored to his father. Your heavenly Father wants you back, and you can be restored to His presence.

God knows that once you have experienced a sincere relationship with Him, you will long for His presence again. He is standing on the porch of eternity and looking down the path of your life, waiting for you to realize, "I need to go home to my Father." As you return, God will not chastise you, because life has already done so. His compassion will embrace you, His righteousness will kiss you, and His peace will envelop you. He will call for a celebration, not a jury, and He will defend you against all who would question His faithfulness and forgiveness.

Healing and wholeness often come to us progressively as we develop and sustain a relationship with the Father through Jesus Christ. Like the father of the Prodigal, God the Father waits for us. He waits while we are disobedient and rebellious. He waits during our seasons of wasted strength and potential. He is long-suffering as we go through periods of trying to find something or someone to replace His voice. He waits for us to come to ourselves, overcome our pride, remember His goodness, rehearse our apology, and come home to His presence. *"Thou wilt show me the path of life: in thy presence is fulness of joy; at thy right hand there are pleasures for evermore"* (Psalm 16:11).

Chapter Seven

Are You Ready to Say Yes?

A vision of wholeness will activate your faith for healing.

The commuter train station was extremely crowded. A problem with the electrical power in another city was creating delays and preventing dozens of travelers—including myself—from getting home. All around me, I could hear the complaints building.

A transit employee had just gone off duty, abandoning the slightly elevated station desk just before the trouble began. I saw his replacement enter from an employee break area. You could just see him thinking, "If I had only called off today, I wouldn't have to deal with this." He was trapped by circumstances, the same as the rest of us, but at least he was getting paid for it.

The transit employee studied the situation. Making what he would soon surely realize was a bad decision, he started making his way through the crowd. When people spotted him, they surged in his direction, and he immediately became the informational bone to a pack of well-dressed wolves. To use another analogy, he was like a running back trying to carry the ball up the middle of a formidable defense. He took an "Excuse me, when will the train be here?" hit every two or three feet. People were acting as if it was his train and his station, and therefore his problem to solve.

When he finally reached the elevated desk, he looked as if he was fighting the inclination to run. It would have been useless, anyway. He had sealed his fate because he was now completely surrounded. Businessmen who were used to getting their way demanded an explanation from him. Their lives were tightly scheduled so, of course, the problem had to have a scheduled time of resolution. Women used all their sweet charm on him, as if he had a train in his vest pocket and their dulcet tones could produce it. Many people kept looking at the information board every thirty seconds, hoping that, by some act of God, the word CANCELLED would suddenly transform into *TRAIN NOW ARRIVING.*

Men started loosening their ties and taking off their jackets, slinging them over their shoulders. A woman pulled out a pair of slippers and put them on. (I wonder how many times she'd had this experience before?) As people stared at her, I couldn't tell whether they were admiring her preparedness or sizing her up to see if they'd be able to wrestle the slippers from her.

Things were getting tense. As if on cue, cell phones leapt out of hiding from coat jackets and purses. Dates were broken, excuses were made, and a few "It's not my fault's" were heard. Several people were emphasizing their points by waving their free hands, as if those on the other ends of the lines could see them.

I spotted a corner to stand in that minimized my exposure to the crowd, so I edged myself past several people and claimed my one square foot of floor. That's when I found myself standing next to Jonathan. We exchanged looks of, "Oh, well," asked where each other was going, then settled in, "sniffing" each other's title, economic status, and education. It soon became clear to me that the train delay was not foremost on Jonathan's mind.

Anchored in Emotional Turmoil

I am continually amazed at how God has a way of scheduling unscheduled meetings in my life. As I talked with Jonathan, I began to realize that his eyes and expression looked wounded. He explained that he had never really talked about his past to anyone else. Then he confided that he had come from a broken home and was still having great difficulty dealing with his father's absence from his life. He was a classic example of someone who has been hurt by his father, as we talked about in a previous chapter. He felt rejected and had tried to submerge the pain by creating an "I'm not going to let anyone else hurt me" mind-set that was designed to protect his heart from being rejected again.

The problem with this mind-set was that it had anchored him for many years in the same place of emotional turmoil. Jonathan anticipated being rejected by others, so he usually did something to sabotage the relationships and circumstances in his life. His negative expectations became self-fulfilling prophecies; He beat others to it and made sure that he was rejected. The more concern that people showed him, the more prone he was to push them away. He had just completed another year of driving away people whom he cared about. In fact, he had recently caused someone very dear to him to leave, doing things that had left the person no other choice. He had grown weary, almost desperate, because he had lived in this way for so many years. He had been stranded emotionally, vocationally, relationally, and spiritually for a long time.

Jonathan believed in God, but his faith didn't go much beyond acknowledging His existence. He apparently hadn't expected God to help him overcome his feelings of abandonment and rejection. He had looked for help from those in his life, but had come to realize that he had surrounded himself with people who were anchored to their own emotional turmoil and therefore had no solutions for him. (I told him that we often attract people who are similar to ourselves, rather than those whom we want to be like.) He had also tried denying his problem, but the internal friction between denial and reality made his struggles even more intense.

> The Father is concerned about our feelings.

Unable to Envision a Different Life

Jonathan had come to see himself only through the distorted lens of his negative life experiences. He felt rejected, lonely, and isolated—and he could not envision his life any differently.

I explained a truth about God that he had never considered: The Father was concerned about his feelings. He thought that God was concerned only with his soul. He didn't understand that his wholeness was as important to God as his salvation. I told him that God never intended for him to be stuck in the same emotional place for the rest of his life. The Lord not only wanted to save him, but also to heal and deliver him from thirty years of emotional captivity so that he could finally live without the wounds and scars of his past. Believing in the existence of God was not enough. Only through receiving God's Son, Jesus Christ, could his heart and mind be healed.

Jonathan said, "I need help. I can't do this alone," so we prayed together, asking Jesus to come into his life. Before that time, I had prayed with people in malls, airports, airplanes, and even cemeteries, but never in a commuter train station at rush hour. Yet even though we were in that crowded station, it was as if we were alone with God.

As we finished the prayer, the transit sign announced that the train was finally coming. I asked Jonathan if I could pray for him again. We bowed our heads once more, and I talked about my disappointment with my own father and the struggle that it had caused in my life. I thanked God that He had given me the strength to be healed of my anger. I told Him that Jonathan's wounds had gone untreated for too long and that his scars needed to be removed. I acknowledged that the Creator had another purpose for Jonathan that included a new vision for his life.

The train announcements came over the intercom, and the crowd began to disperse. Jonathan would be catching the same train that he had always taken, but he was headed in an entirely new direction in his life.

Seeing beyond Your Pain

One of the hindrances to being healed without scars is not being able to see beyond your present circumstances or state of mind. Perhaps you are like Jonathan, unable to envision a life without emotional pain. Years of distress can take their toll, as we see in the story of a lame man who had been sick for almost forty years.

> *Now there is in Jerusalem by the Sheep Gate a pool, which is called in Hebrew, Bethesda, having five porches. In these lay a great multitude of sick people, blind, lame, paralyzed, waiting for the moving of the water. For an angel went down at a certain time into the pool and stirred up the water; then whoever stepped in first, after the stirring of the water, was made well of whatever disease he had. Now a certain man was there who had an infirmity thirty-eight years. When Jesus saw him lying there, and knew that he already had been in that condition a long time, He said to him, "Do you want to be made well?"* (John 5:2–6 NKJV)

Why do you think that Jesus asked him if he wanted to be healed when it seems obvious that he needed it? Perhaps He wanted to test how much the man really wanted to be restored. You can be in a bad condition for so long that you can become complacent or even content in it. When God wants to take your pain from you, you struggle with Him for it. You're in a tug of war about it. Why? You've been thinking and talking about your pain for so long that you've tied your identity to it. You are afraid that if you lost it, you would no longer know yourself. Or perhaps you think you don't deserve any better.

You are afraid that if you lose your pain, you will no longer know yourself.

God is asking you to see beyond your pain. This doesn't have as much to do with the person or event that caused the pain as it does the feelings of loss, hurt, and failure that are associated with the situation. These feelings are what you keep replaying in your heart and mind, and they are limiting your outlook. What should have been a short-term issue has become a full-fledged lifestyle for you.

A Problem of Perception

Jesus encountered a woman whose affliction limited her ability to see beyond her circumstances.

Now [Jesus] *was teaching in one of the synagogues on the Sabbath. And behold, there was a woman who had a spirit of infirmity eighteen years, and was bent over and could in no way raise herself up. But when Jesus saw her, He called her to Him and said to her, "Woman, you are loosed from your infirmity." And He laid His hands on her, and immediately she was made straight, and glorified God....*[Jesus said,] *"So ought not this woman, being a daughter of Abraham, whom Satan has bound; think of it; for eighteen years, be loosed from this bond?"* (Luke 13:10–13, 16 NKJV)

This woman had a *"spirit of infirmity"* for eighteen years. As the affliction progressed, she became bowed over. Her problem was stronger than her ability to raise herself up. That's the case with many of us. If we were to look through the eyes of Jesus, we would see that our spirits are *"bent over."* The weight of past trauma keeps us from standing up straight in the face of life. It has taken the edge off our power for living.

The woman with the spirit of affliction is a symbol of limited vision. Her head was being drawn closer to her feet every year. She was being drawn toward herself so that, probably, all she could do was think about her problem. After eighteen years, the people in this woman's synagogue had gotten used to seeing her in a bent-over state, and she also had gotten used to it. Is there something in your life that is weighing you down so that you can't see anything except your hurt and pain?

Perhaps you can think back to the very day you were first afflicted. You even know what the weather was like and what

> Is there something weighing you down so you can't see past the pain?

you were wearing at the time. Now you can't take as much stress as you used to because the emotional toll has drained your resilience. It has changed the way you see things. Perhaps the trauma has altered your life's course or stopped you in your tracks so that you can't make any progress.

"Do You Want to Be Made Well?"

If you are to be healed, you must understand the liberating truth that Jonathan discovered: God didn't intend for you to remain anchored in the same emotional place for the rest of your life. Notice that Jesus calls the woman a *"daughter of Abraham"* (Luke 13:16). Abraham symbolizes true faith, so Jesus' designation of her indicates that she was a woman of genuine faith who was suffering affliction. Jesus loves her—bent and all—and He wants to set her free. He wants to set you free, too. He wants you to be whole, complete, and able to live life to the fullest. He desires that you enjoy His blessings as you live in His love, power, promise, and purpose.

You've been emotionally imprisoned for long enough. You're controlled by other's opinions of you. You lean on your own understanding in regard to what you are capable of accomplishing in life—yet that understanding has been distorted by fear or rejection. Your emotions constantly run the gamut from hot to cold, happy to sad. It's time to get off the roller coaster because chaos is not your legacy. You haven't been saved to live in bondage.

Jesus asks us the same question that He asked the lame man in John 5:6, *"Do you want to be made well?"* (NKJV). In other words, "Are you ready to say yes to your healing?" Jesus was asking the lame man, in effect, "How do you see yourself? Do you want a restoration of your dominion, of God's original plan for your life? Do you want your power, authority, strength, and will back? Do you want to walk in healing and in resurrection power? Do you want to be whole and complete?" Jesus' words give us vision for our lives because, suddenly, we see things from His perspective, and what seemed impossible becomes possible.

Again, the problems we face are not the real issue; it's how we *feel* about these problems that causes us distress. When a problem seems greater than God's ability to solve it, we need a change of perception. *"The spirit of wisdom and revelation"* (Ephesians 1:17) is available to transfer our faith in the problem to faith in God. When our faith is transformed, our relationship with Him is also altered, positioning us for the healing of our wounds and the removal of our scars.

> Are you ready to say yes to your healing?

Vision versus Sight

To understand how to live by God's vision for our lives and not our present circumstances, we must recognize that there is a difference between vision and sight. Sight involves focusing with the natural eye on what is visible. It gives us the power to confirm our physical reality. The problem is that, for many of us, sight has become our *only* means of confirming reality. We want to believe only what we see, just like the apostle Thomas.

After hearing that the other disciples had seen the resurrected Jesus, Thomas replied, *"Except I shall see in his hands the print of the nails, and put my finger into the print of the nails, and thrust my hand into his side, I will not believe"* (John 20:25). Reality was confirmed by sight when Jesus appeared to Thomas and said, *"Reach hither thy finger, and behold my hands; and reach hither thy hand, and thrust it into my side: and be not faithless, but believing"* (v. 27).

Vision is not like sight. It confirms an unseen reality. Jesus said to Thomas, *"Because thou hast seen me, thou hast believed: blessed are they that have **not seen, and yet have believed**"* (v. 29, emphasis added). Vision confirms a reality that, for the moment, exists in the spiritual realm or imagination but will eventually be manifested. It is the ability to conceive of something that you can't see with your natural eyes. With sight, we say, "I'll believe it when I see it," but with vision, we say, "I believe it, even though I can't yet see it." For example, it is vision that gives you the capacity to imagine a house with blue shutters, drapes in the windows, a two-car garage, and a flag on the porch blowing in the wind, even though your dream house has not yet been built. A vision is a view that is so vivid it evokes an emotional response. It gets you excited about what will come to pass.

> We must recognize that there is a difference between vision and sight.

We begin to understand vision when we recognize that we really do traverse between two realities: a physical one and a spiritual one—the one that we were born into and the one that we were born again into. Vision confirms a higher spiritual reality. Years of wounding and scarring block our ability to see ourselves the way God sees us. In our pain, we see only our physical or human reality, and that is why we lose our focus and power for living.

Since vision enables you to experience something in your mind's eye that you've not yet experienced as a physical reality, it is vision that will allow you to see yourself healed and delivered even before your circumstances have changed. The faith that this vision activates will prepare the way for your restoration.

A Vision for Your Healing

Vision is powerful because it connects us with the mind of God. What we are experiencing on earth right now is real, but God has another "now" for us. He sees us living above our hindrances and circumstances. He sees us delivered and walking in joy and power.

How do we rise from our view of ourselves into God's view? Visions are usually mind-blowing because they are so different from our present knowledge, experience, and expectations. Any time you receive a real vision from God, the Holy Spirit must communicate it to your spirit first because your mind won't be able to comprehend it. The spirit must rule the mind so that, once we have the vision, we exercise faith in it and don't allow what we experience in our physical or emotional environments to control what we think.

> The content of every true vision is the Word of God.

The key is this: The content of every true vision is the Word of God. The promise of God, activated in our hearts by the power of the Holy Spirit, is the seed of our visions. Vision acknowledges these two things: First, through faith in God's

Word, I recognize that there is a reality I had not previously seen. Second, if I keep heading in the direction of my vision, I will see it come to fruition.

God speaks His purposes for your life in the Scripture. One of the most powerful examples of this is in Luke 4:18:

> [Jesus said,] *The Spirit of the Lord is upon me, because he hath anointed me to preach the gospel to the poor; he hath sent me to heal the brokenhearted, to preach deliverance to the captives, and recovering of sight to the blind, to set at liberty them that are bruised.*

When you acknowledge and accept His Word, your mind begins to be transformed, so that now your thoughts are aligned with His. The content of your vision is not what *you* think. It is what *God* thinks. Therefore, as you read the Scripture, you will see how He views you and what He desires for your life, and then your vision for your healing will be enlarged.

If someone tells you something about your life, it must confirm what God has already said in His Word. What we tell ourselves also has to be built on His promises. We have to learn to allow our visions to control what we say about ourselves and our situations. As long as we know how God sees us, then we can affirm that our present negative circumstances are temporary. When we start conducting ourselves according to the vision, and not according to our adverse situations, we sow positive seeds into our spirits.

This approach is not a willful denial of reality. We have to learn how to sow positive seeds even while recognizing the negative aspects of our circumstances. We're not avoiding what is wrong, but rather confirming that we have the answer for it. We can tell ourselves, "This is who I am now, but God says that He's going to make me into something new."

"Believe Ye That I Am Able to Do This?"

After we begin to understand the way God sees us, Jesus asks us another question: "Do you believe that I am able to heal you?" This is the same question that He asked two blind men who sought Him for healing:

When Jesus departed thence, two blind men followed him, crying, and saying, Thou son of David, have mercy on us. And when he was come into the house, the blind men came to him: and Jesus saith unto them, Believe ye that I am able to do this? They said unto him, Yea, Lord. Then touched he their eyes, saying, According to your faith be it unto you. And their eyes were opened. (Matthew 9:27–30)

Time and desperation often partner to produce great prayer and faith. The two blind men had been trapped in the same position day after day. Their blindness not only took their sight, but also clouded their vision for the future. Like the lame man, they probably had become resigned to their affliction, so that they were unable to imagine themselves seeing. But then they heard that Jesus had life-changing power, and they sought Him out. When they found Him, they began to cry out with persistence, *"Have mercy on us."* They also worshipped Him and acknowledged His Lordship by calling Him *"Son of David."*

> "You may believe that I *am*, but do you believe that I am *able*?"

The question Jesus asked them was intended to produce vision and build faith in them. He was inquiring, "You may believe that I *am,* but do you believe that I am *able*—able to establish joy where there is pain, strength where there is weakness, prosperity where there is brokenness?" The question is like a pianist striking a note on a piano. The music in the instrument is dormant until the key is struck. Likewise, Jesus' words struck a chord in the blind men, activating their dormant faith for deliverance, and they answered Him, "Yes, I believe You can!"

Instead of hoping in things and people who cannot help us, we have to come to the same point of faith where we can say, "Lord, all I want is to have a vision for what You desire for my life. All I want is to be healed and delivered as You have said in Your Word."

The Bible says, *"Faith cometh by hearing, and hearing by the word of God"* (Romans 10:17). The blind men's faith was stirred by the living Word, and it became active as they began to move away from a mind-set of blindness and into the purpose of God for their lives. Without faith, the power of heaven would not have been available to them, and their miracle would have lain dormant. Because of their faith, they were linked to God's power, healing, and deliverance. They saw themselves seeing again, and their vision became reality.

"The Evidence of Things Not Seen"

"Faith is the substance of things hoped for, the evidence of things not seen" (Hebrews 11:1). When you have faith, you have not yet seen the fulfillment of your vision, but you are anticipating it. Just as Abraham believed God's promise that he would have a child, and then lived to see that promise fulfilled, you will see your healing and deliverance as you have faith in God's promises for you. *"It was not through law that Abraham and his offspring*

received the promise that he would be heir of the world, but through the righteousness that comes by faith" (Romans 4:13 NIV). The only way you get attached to the promises is by faith. Genesis 15:6 says, "[Abraham] *believed in the LORD* [in the vision that God had promised him]; *and he counted it to him for righteousness."*

Abraham is the forerunner of all those who would believe in the promises of God. He believed God for what he couldn't physically see but knew in his spirit was real. He had a vision of it. *"Therefore it is of faith, that it might be by grace; to the end the promise might be sure to all the seed; not to that only which is of the law, but to that also which is of the faith of Abraham; who is the father of us all"* (Romans 4:16). The fulfillment of the promise is certain for *"all the seed"*—and you are the seed if you have put your trust in God and been made righteous through faith in Jesus Christ.

Abraham was challenged by the fact that there were many years between the promise of a son and its fulfillment in Isaac. His expectation was severely tested, but the Word of God came to him, and his expectation was resurrected.

> [Abraham,] *contrary to hope* [expectation], *in hope* [expectation] *believed, so that he became the father of many nations, according to what was spoken, "So shall your descendants be." And not being weak in faith, he did not consider his own body, already dead (since he was about a hundred years old), and the deadness of Sarah's womb. He did not waver at the promise of God through unbelief, but was strengthened in faith, giving glory to God, and being fully convinced that what He had promised He was also able to perform.* (vv. 18–21 NKJV)

There are things in our lives that are dead. No matter how hard we try, we can't seem to get them to work. But the

Bible says that *"God...gives life to the dead and calls those things which do not exist* [do not presently exist] *as though they did"* (v. 17 NKJV). Abraham believed that, even though his body and Sarah's womb were as good as dead, it didn't matter because He who made the promise was able to fulfill it. He considered what was unseen to be real because he believed what God had told him and knew that God could bring into being what he couldn't produce in his own power.

Do you believe in the reality of God's Word? The Father doesn't want you to think of the Scripture as mere words on paper, but as a living reality. He wants you to place the wounding and scarring reality of the past next to His Word and choose to believe what He says. He desires to do the seeming impossible by helping you to see not only your physical reality, but also the reality of faith. The Scripture says, *"If ye abide in me, and my words abide in you, ye shall ask what ye will, and it shall be done* [granted] *unto you"* (John 15:7), and *"Eye hath not seen, nor ear heard, neither have entered into the heart of man, the things which God hath prepared for them that love him"* (1 Corinthians 2:9).

> The God who made the promise is able to fulfill it.

The Jericho Directive

Sometimes, although we want to say yes to Jesus' questions, "Do you want to be made well?" and "Do you believe that I am able to do this?" something keeps blocking our vision. I call this type of hindrance a "Jericho."

The city of Jericho, which the Israelites had to defeat in order to enter into the Promised Land, symbolizes the strongholds that must be conquered in our lives before we can see and possess God's promises. Once they are pulled down, a new reality can be released. What do I mean by a Jericho? Whatever is contrary to the nature and Word of God. For example, unforgiveness toward those who have wronged you, hatred for yourself or someone else, and jealousy are all types of Jerichos that can block your vision.

As long as Jerichos are in our way, we won't be able to see or experience our destinies. We'll be trying to envision the future through walls of sin and doubt. You may be asking yourself, "Can I conquer the Jerichos in my life?" In other words, you are acknowledging, *"I know that nothing good lives in me, that is, in my sinful nature. For I have the desire to do what is good, but I cannot carry it out"* (Romans 7:18 NIV).

Israel's defeat of Jericho is an illustration to us that only spiritual weapons can bring down barriers to the fulfillment of vision. The people of God could not defeat Jericho by fighting a conventional battle. They had to follow God's directive, which was to march around Jericho, blow trumpets, and shout. In the same way, your Jericho is a place where your experience or strength will not help you. It must be conquered by faith in God and His Word.

God's directive for your situation may seem as unusual as His instruction to Israel. This is because it will seem contrary to your nature. But it will be consistent with His nature. You are going to have to believe what He says, no matter how unusual it seems, if you are to receive healing. This is so you will know that only God has the power to heal you. Again, the essence of the Jericho directive was this: Spiritual strongholds cannot be defeated by might or power, but only by the Holy Spirit. The Bible says,

> *(For the weapons of our warfare are not carnal, but mighty through God to the pulling down of strong holds;) casting*

down imaginations, and every high thing that exalteth itself against the knowledge of God, and bringing into captivity every thought to the obedience of Christ.

(2 Corinthians 10:4–5)

The problem of blocked vision is identified here as *"imaginations"* or reasoning. The stronghold is in our thoughts and emotions. The enemy's intention is to take the material of the negative circumstances in our lives and build Jerichos in our minds and hearts so that we will remain outside the promises. We have to counteract his strategy by bringing our perceptions, thoughts, and ideas into alignment with God's Word.

Living in God's Reality

Your past wounds have produced scars that have given you a distorted outlook on your present life and future possibilities. This entrenched mind-set has functioned like a locked door, barring you from the fulfilling life that God has promised you. You have to get to the point where you start saying, "I can't do it, but I know that God has it under control. Because of His promises, I can see my healing."

By faith, you must capture a vision of yourself as released from the place where you have been anchored in your emotions, a vision of yourself healed without scars from the wounds of life, a vision of yourself fulfilling your purpose and living in God's provision. The Lord has already spoken in His Word concerning your healing. The decision is yours. I invite you to live in the reality of God, to live above your circumstances by faith. Are you ready to say, "Yes, Lord, I want to be healed, and I believe that You are able to do this"? Jesus is always available and willing to heal you of the scars of your past.

Chapter Eight

Praise Is Part of the Process

*Praise leads to a renewed expectation
of the fulfillment of God's promise.*

One of the minor irritations of life is a forced layover at an airport. If you have to endure a layover, however, Charlotte International Airport in North Carolina is the place to be. I call it the "rocking chair" airport because you can sit and watch the parade go by: When I've been there, bands have been playing and people have been singing. I've also discovered unique food outlets tucked away in surprising places. (You need all that after going through customs on a busy day!)

On one trip, I arrived at the Charlotte airport in order to catch a connecting flight. Like most of the passengers, I had hurried to disembark the plane, but, for me, it was a rush to nowhere. I didn't need to hurry because I'd be sitting for a while in the waiting area at the gate for my next flight. Little did I know that God had another connection in mind for me during my downtime in Charlotte. He had scheduled a meeting with the woman sitting next to me.

Lost Praise

Celia was a Christian, but she had lost any expectation that something positive would occur in her life. As a result, she had lost her praise for God. What did she have to thank Him for? Her heart's desire was to have a loving family relationship, but this desire had been marred by the abuse she had suffered from her father earlier in life. The abuse led to an emotional and physical journey that had become increasingly hopeless. She had allowed herself to enter a series of relationships that were always highly sexual and volatile. On several occasions, she'd fought the urge to commit suicide. She felt that the pattern of her life—including the kind of people she was attracted to as well as those who were attracted to her—would never change. Year after year, as she had fueled her loss of hope and self-esteem with more and more destructive experiences, her expectations had continually diminished. After almost forty years, she was still feeling the same pain, guilt, and hopelessness that she had always felt, only it was multiplied many times over.

As we sat and talked, Celia began to question me about God and the Bible. I asked her if she loved her current significant other, and she described a relationship filled with positive references. Yet these references were limited to the very beginning of the relationship: She had fond memories of their first meeting, their first conversation, and their first date, with birds singing and music playing. Once she had become involved with the man, however, the tone of their relationship had changed drastically. Yet, in her mind, the initial blush of the relationship validated her reasons for staying in it.

Celia hadn't lost her purpose; she had never felt that she had one. She had spent so much of her life trying to appeal to men that she had not developed as a person. Her only validation was in her ability to attract men, but her relationships always ended badly. Celia realized while talking to me that she felt hollow inside. With every negative experience that she had allowed herself to become involved in, she had become more hopeless. What it came down to was that she'd been futilely chasing a feeling of love. Yet, feelings of love are not caught; they are developed as a relationship grows in a healthy way.

> Celia hadn't lost her purpose; she had never felt that she had one.

As I helped her to recognize the common threads in all her relationships, she continually blamed the men for her loss of hope and self-esteem. As many people do, she never accepted responsibility for her situation. None of the problems of her present life were her fault. She had repeatedly made the same poor choices, and those decisions had become the scars of her experience. The only way she could excuse her choices was to think of herself as a perpetual victim.

Celia had suffered deep wounds—some were inflicted upon her and some were self-inflicted. I told her that, of course, the early abuse by her father was not her fault. He had hurt her when he should have protected her. The reason she continued to suffer and make wrong choices, however, was that she had transferred that lack of responsibility to her actions as an adult. She had connected the dots in her life and come up with an explanation for her pain, but they were the wrong dots. She was honest about her past experiences, but she continued to allow those experiences to fuel her present behavior.

Misdirected Expectations

I began to connect the dots for her in a different way. I explained that she had aimed her expectations in the wrong direction. She had a certain faith in God, but she had put her hopes in people. She had been waiting for a knight in shining armor to gallop into her life and rescue her. I told her that her true Rescuer had already written, called, and come to see her, but she had missed or ignored His advances. That Man was Jesus. He had been seeking her, and He alone had the power to mend her heart and remove the scars.

> Jesus had been seeking her, and He alone had the power to mend her heart.

As we talked, the Holy Spirit gave me insights beyond my natural ability, and I began to replay her life as if I had been there—asking her questions that no one had ever asked and giving her the answers that she needed from the Word of God. In the midst of the darkness of her reality, I saw that there was a spark of faith in her; I knew that she had faith enough to be healed.

I talked to her about the preserving grace of God. The most amazing thing about her life, I explained, was that she had survived all her negative experiences. The devil has no mercy in his toolkit. He had tried to destroy her mind and her very life, but God had kept her safe until she was ready to receive her healing.

Celia was unable to comprehend God's vision for her life: She was convinced that He didn't want her any longer, so she had no expectation of His love or acceptance of her, let alone His power to heal her. The primary work of the Holy Spirit in us, after regeneration, is personal wholeness. To move toward wholeness, we require a personal revelation of God's purposes for us, so I told her again that Jesus had been looking for her. His ministry was to look for people who were wounded. He came to seek and save the lost. (See Luke 19:10.) He came looking for those who were fractured by life.

A Time for Deliverance

When Celia caught a glimpse of God's purpose for her, she began to thank Him. She recognized that God had preserved her through all her struggles and shame. He had a plan for her life, and He would not be satisfied until His purpose for her was fulfilled. I began to speak to the wounded and fallen places in her life, affirming that, although she had undergone relentless emotional attack, she had lived. She had taken the enemy's best shot and endured. Yes, she had participated in her own chaos and confusion, but she was alive because God had preserved her for this day in order to hear His Word and purpose. Celia recognized that this was the moment of rescue that she'd been waiting for. It was time for her to be delivered from her pain and shame.

> God has a plan for your life, and He won't be satisfied until His purpose for you is fulfilled.

I then asked Celia the same question that I have asked hundreds of people who struggle with similar issues: "What do you love about the person you are with, and when did you stop loving yourself?" Her eyes lost focus. She was looking into her past. Then something within her broke dramatically. She could feel the place and the time; she could see the precise moment that she had stopped loving herself. That was the beginning of her healing. For the first time in years, she began to give God heartfelt praise for extending to her His faithfulness and love even when she didn't love herself.

She finally realized that her expectations had been misdirected. She had put her hopes in people when they should have been in God, and this had perpetuated the downward spiral of her life. Now her expectation had changed, and whenever expectation is transferred to God, praise is resurrected. She knew that she could look to Him to provide the love and security that she lacked. She could receive healing in her emotions and renewed hope for her life.

Celia had stopped at the airport to change planes, but it was her life that was transformed. The baggage of her past was about to be lost forever. She would not be filing a claim to get those bags back!

Have You Lost Your Expectation?

Life's disappointments can cause our faith to waver and our hopes to fade. Have you lost your expectation for a close relationship with God? Have you given up hope of a happy and healthy marriage? Do you no longer anticipate a fulfilling job or vocation? We often lose our expectations when we undergo testing or trials, and life no longer looks good to us. We slowly slide into less than the best for ourselves when we seek easy comfort from life's challenges, when we lose sight of God's love and power, and when we lose faith in our own worth.

There have been times in all our lives when our praise has been negatively affected by a loss of expectation. When we lose the anticipation of good in our lives, we stop praising

God because we no longer feel thankful for what He has done and will do for us. Yet when we cut off our praise, we also cut off the flow of life from our Source of true hope. We end up being wounded and scarred by our experiences instead of being upheld in them by the presence of the Father.

A Mind-Set of Captivity

In a previous chapter, we saw that the Israelites built a golden calf to worship as their god—even after the living God had powerfully delivered them from slavery and the Egyptian army. The calf represented both their life in captivity and the false mind-set of their captors. How could they have turned away from God so quickly? Their attitudes and actions were based on insecurity. They wanted God to prove Himself to them over and over when He had already demonstrated His power and love and had promised to take care of them.

> We stop praising God because we no longer feel thankful for what He has done.

First, the Israelites became insecure about a lack of food and water in the desert. Then Moses went up into a high mountain and spent an extended time with God, and they grew nervous about the apparent absence of leadership in the camp. Doubting both God and the leader that He had provided, they built a calf using the gold that the defeated Egyptians had given to them when they had left the country. They turned the very thing that represented God's abundance to them into an idol. This is because the Israelites were still carrying in their hearts the mind-set of their captivity. Even though they were physically free, their hearts were still enslaved.

The "calf" of their negative experience of slavery manifested itself in times of testing and trial. The Israelites' murmuring in the wilderness about the seeming comforts of captivity, and their creation of an idol on which to focus their attention, reveal a loss of expectation in their lives. They quickly abandoned their vision of serving the loving and powerful living God and reduced themselves to relying on a mere statue made by their own hands. Years later, God asked their descendents,

> I remember...the devotion of your youth, the love of your betrothals, your following after Me in the wilderness, through a land not sown....What injustice did your fathers find in Me, that they went far from Me and walked after emptiness and became empty? And they did not say, "Where is the LORD who brought us up out of the land of Egypt, who led us through the wilderness, through a land of deserts and of pits, through a land of drought and of deep darkness, through a land that no one crossed and where no man dwelt?" (Jeremiah 2:2, 5–6 NASB)

The Scripture says, "As [a man] *thinketh in his heart, so is he*" (Proverbs 23:7). The Israelites were scarred by their captivity, and their slavery mind-set prevented them from expecting more than an empty life. It also drained the praise right out of them. They didn't give the Lord the love, honor, and worship that He deserved. When they lost their expectation, they were reduced to worshiping a worthless idol. The result was that they lost their own worth.

Lowering Your Standards

A loss of worth occurs when you lower the standard of what you find acceptable for your life. This doesn't mean that God values you any less. It means that you've robbed yourself of living according to God's Spirit and ways. As the years pass, you continually lower the standard so that, finally, you end up with no standards at all. Like many people, perhaps you don't realize that you have to alter your perception of yourself when you continually compromise who you truly are.

As Celia discovered, involvement in negative relationships often tends to diminish our expectations. You start off having high standards for your relationship, but as the relationship becomes abusive or exploitative, your standards of love must lower if you're going to stay in it. As the abuse and exploitation continue, you must further lower your expectations to the point where you may begin taking personal responsibility for the abuse, saying, "It's my fault that he's treating me in this way. I must be doing something to anger him." As time goes on, you abandon your desire for a positive future by further lowering your hopes. You begin the time game: "I have invested too much time in this relationship to leave now."

Negative circumstances can create very strong emotional bonds. By the time you finally realize that you are dwelling in a destructive situation, pride and sacrifice have usually killed your expectations for a healthy relationship. You are too proud to leave because others have advised you to break off the relationship, and you haven't listened to their counsel. You've already sacrificed your self-respect to maintain the relationship, and you feel that the other person can't live without you and therefore you have to stay to help him or her.

Celia kept getting into destructive relationships because she did not think that there was anything better for her. Even when good things would happen to her, she would build a "golden calf" and return to her abusive roots. She continued to stray from positive circumstances while being drawn to exploitative ones until faith and hope were reawakened in her life.

Let's look at how we can keep our expectation for healing and deliverance strong, no matter what situations we may face.

Our Expectation Is in God— Wait Only on Him

First, we must discover how to encourage ourselves during testings and trials so that we can maintain our spiritual and emotional strength. In the most critical personal times, it is not unusual to find yourself facing your problems alone—whether you are surrounded by people or not. Isolation forces you to look toward God in situations where those whom you expect to help can only offer words of temporary comfort. This is actually a good thing, because there are some things that only God can do.

> **God alone is the One who can save and deliver you.**

David talked about this truth in Psalm 62. He expressed an urgency and a determination that nobody but God had an answer to his need.

> *Truly my soul waiteth upon God: from him cometh my salvation. He only is my rock and my salvation; he is my defence; I shall not be greatly moved....**My soul, wait thou only upon God; for my expectation is from him**. He only is my rock and my salvation: he is my defence; I shall not be moved. In God is my salvation and my glory: the rock of my strength, and my refuge, is in God. Trust in him at all times; ye people, pour out your heart before him: God is a refuge for us.* (Psalm 62:1–2, 5–8, emphasis added)

Through the struggles of his life, David discovered that God alone is the One who could save and deliver him. You

146

have to learn how to encourage yourself in the Lord, as David did. As your dependence on God increases, your focus shifts from your problem, from other people, and from your past, to Him. You realize that He has always been with you. The peace of God then begins to push aside your pain, and joy returns. These things signal the resurrection of praise in your life, which will lift you above your problems.

All our expectation should ultimately rest in God. He is the source of our deliverance. The answer to our prayers doesn't begin with us. It begins with Him. When the revelation of God's protective custody becomes a reality in our lives, we acknowledge that He alone is our unfailing help and strength. This happens because faith renews our expectation—and expectation becomes the catalyst for heartfelt praise.

> As your dependence on God increases, your focus shifts from your problem to Him.

When Expectation Is Lost

The story of the Shunammite woman in 2 Kings 4 is an illustration of how we can respond to situations when our expectation is threatened or lost. This woman probably had great hopes for her life. Her husband was capable and provided her with life's comforts. Because he was a man of wealth and influence, she enjoyed great status among her peers. The only thing that she didn't have was a child. The Scripture says that her husband was old, implying that, by this time, he may not have been capable of producing a child.

The Hebrews believed that conception was a blessing from God, but after many years of childlessness, the Shunammite woman did not expect this blessing. She possessed most of the things that other people desired, but the one thing she wanted, God had not provided.

The prophet Elisha came to Shunem and passed by her house, and she perceived that he was anointed. Even though she had not received the blessing of a child, she apparently still loved and honored God and desired to help His servants. She urged Elisha to come in and refresh himself with a meal. After that, every time he came through Shunem, he stopped at the woman's house to eat. Then the woman and her husband built Elisha a room to rest in whenever he was in town.

One day, touched by the woman's generosity, Elisha asked her what he could do for her to repay her kindness. When she replied that she had everything she needed, Elisha's servant, Gehazi, reminded him of her childlessness. Elisha told the woman that God would give her a child by the same time the next year. This news was beyond her expectations, and she told Elisha not to give her false hope. But Elisha's words came true, and the woman had a baby boy the next year. Several years passed, and one day the woman's son complained of a severe headache and died in her arms.

It sometimes happens that we receive a promise from God and rejoice, only to despair later when it seems as if that promise is lost. When this woman's expectation for a child was rekindled and then seemingly extinguished, she did not give up but ran to the source of her hope. She placed her child's body on the bed in Elisha's guest room and then hurriedly traveled to where Elisha was, fell down at his feet, and said, *"Did I desire a son of my lord? did I not say, Do not deceive me?"* (2 Kings 2:28). Elisha acted quickly and went to the boy and prayed, and God raised the boy up and restored him to his mother. (See 2 Kings 4:8–37.)

Pour Out Your Lost Hopes to God

When the Shunammite woman faced a threat to her hope, she poured out her heart to the prophet, who represented God to the people of Israel, and her hope was restored. Similarly, our wholeness and restoration begin as we pour out our issues before our heavenly Father. We can go directly to Him and trust Him to hear us because the Scripture says that the righteous can run boldly to God in troubled times. *"Let us therefore come boldly unto the throne of grace, that we may obtain mercy, and find grace to help in time of need"* (Hebrews 4:16).

The heavenly Father is our *"hiding place"* (Psalm 32:7; 119:114). He is a refuge when things seem out of control and life appears poised to deliver another blow. The Bible says that God stabilizes us during tough times. *"I have set the LORD always before me: because he is at my right hand, I shall not be moved"* (Psalm 16:8). Friends and loved ones might be changeable, opportunities might be missed, difficulties may challenge us, but God is always faithful.

> When you give God your ruins, He gives you His restoration.

When you present the wounds and scars of life to God in prayer, He speaks to you according to His nature and character. You say, "Lord, I can't bear these wounds another day," and He says, *"I am the LORD that healeth thee"* (Exodus 15:26). You say, "I can't make it without You," and He says, *"I will never leave thee, nor forsake thee"* (Hebrews 13:5). You say, "Lord, I'm depressed," and He says that He is *"the lifter up of* [your] *head"* (Psalm 3:3). When you give Him your ruins, He gives you His restoration. His power and kingdom are activated in us, loosening the enemy's grip while readjusting our view of our problems.

Focusing on God Resurrects Praise

As God encourages you, the next step of your deliverance is praise. When you begin to think about God's nature and goodness, you remember who He is and what He's done for you. You can't help thanking Him, and your praise is resurrected. You recall other times when circumstances stole your expectation and robbed you of your praise, and how He restored you. When you think about the love of God and the unfailing promises in His Word, your faith is renewed, and the seeds of expectation are sown. Expectation gives birth to a praise that waits for God to move. *"My soul, wait thou only upon God; for my expectation is from him"* (Psalm 62:5).

Sometimes, our faith isn't as strong as we think it is when we have to wait longer than we want to for what we are expecting. Our situations seem unchanging and our prayers don't appear to be a priority with God. Yet, when our expectation is truly in Him, we always have a praise on reserve for Him because we know that He is faithful.

God Is Present in Our Praises

In an earlier chapter, we talked about the power of the presence of God in our lives. When trouble comes, we often stop praising, but in doing so, we remove ourselves from the presence of the only One who can help us. The Scripture says that God *"inhabitest the praises of Israel* [His people]*"* (Psalm 22:3), or is *"enthroned upon the praises of Israel* [His people]*"* (NASB). Praise is a form of communication with God. The language of praise invites His response and very present help. In praise, our perception of the intimacy and intensity of God's presence is increased. When we praise God with sincerity, we can know that He is with us and will be our strength and refuge.

Because God dwells in your praises, as you worship Him, He moves into the very center of your wounds and scars. Whatever the disappointments of life have made insufficient in you cannot remain in that condition. Insufficiency is impossible in the presence of God. Any condition that seeks to block your joy cannot remain the same when He is there because the Bible says, *"In thy presence is fulness of joy"* (Psalm 16:11). There is no greater power than God's power. When He inhabits your praise, He moves into your emotional, spiritual, and physical needs to bring healing and restoration.

God doesn't just visit your wounds; He inhabits the cause and the condition of them. He doesn't just see your scars; He pours the oil of His Spirit on them. When the scars are removed, then your faith is affirmed and your expectation is resurrected. Therefore, praise both causes us to have faith and expectation and also springs from them once we are in possession of them again. This is what I call "the cycle of praise."

> Insufficiency is impossible in the presence of God.

A Continuous Habit

Praise is most effective when it is habitual. We read in Psalms, *"I will sing unto the LORD as long as I live: I will sing praise to my God while I have my being"* (Psalm 104:33), and *"While I live will I praise the LORD: I will sing praises unto my God while I have any being"* (Psalm 146:2). Praise is a spiritual weapon sharpened by use in good times so that it will be readily available and effective when times are difficult. The battle for your complete wholeness will never be won with human weapons. *"For the weapons of our warfare are not carnal, but mighty through*

God to the pulling down of strong holds" (2 Corinthians 10:4). The most effective weapons are spiritual. They have the power to mend your emotional wounds and remove the strongholds of scarring in your life.

David understood that praise should be a regular part of our daily lives. He said, *"I will bless the LORD at all times: his praise shall continually be in my mouth"* (Psalm 34:1). This speaks of his willful determination to give God praise no matter what situation he was facing. There are times when we don't necessarily feel like praising God. Again, periods of great stress divert our attention from God to the difficulties that we are facing. Our problems begin to appear greater than God's ability to handle them. It is in these critical times that we, like David, must have a determination to praise God.

> The battle will never be won with human weapons.

Each time you make a commitment to have your wounds healed and your scars removed, the enemy will raise opposition to hinder the transformation. Sometimes, the same situations or circumstances that you believed God for in the past will present themselves with greater strength than ever before. Your deliverance is being challenged. As the enemy seeks to discourage you, you must encourage yourself with praise concerning the faithfulness of God's promises.

The psalmist was at a low point, close to failure, when he said, *"Unless the LORD had been my help, my soul would soon have settled in silence. If I say, 'My foot slips,' Your mercy, O LORD, will hold me up. In the multitude of my anxieties within me, Your comforts delight my soul"* (Psalm 94:17–19 NKJV). Praise is a chief weapon against depression. As you contemplate your problem, you often embark on a downward emotional path, and the resulting depression disrupts your peace. Since praise requires that you focus your mind on the goodness of God, it moves your thoughts from the depressing to the uplifting.

A No-Matter-What Praise

The habit of praise will not fail us during the tests and trials that we all must face. Let's look at the example of Job in the Old Testament. It seems clear that he had developed a habit of praise before his troubles began. The Bible describes him as a man who was *"perfect and upright, and one that feared God, and eschewed evil"* (Job 1:1). He was devoted to God and prayed continually on behalf of his family (v. 5). Not only was he faithful, but he had also been blessed with great wealth (v 3).

This peaceful life is interrupted when Satan goes before God and accuses Job of having a false agenda of serving God only because he has been wonderfully blessed with wealth and honor. God allows Satan to test Job—within certain limits. In one day, Job loses almost all that God has given him: his ten children as well as everything he owns. Only his wife and a few of his servants survive. Job's first reaction is to praise God, saying, *"Naked came I out of my mother's womb, and naked shall I return thither* [I came into the world with nothing, and I will leave with nothing]: *the LORD gave, and the LORD hath taken away; blessed be the name of the LORD"* (Job 1:21).

When Satan next afflicts Job with boils, his wife is amazed that he has not changed his testimony concerning God. She asks him why he is holding on to his faith and tells him, *"Curse God, and die"* (Job 2:9). He answers, in effect, "What! Should I praise Him only when things are going well?" (See verse 10.)

Then Job's friends show up to find fault with him, even though he has done nothing wrong. In the midst of all this,

Job gives God praise and expresses his desire to be in His presence.

> *For I know that my Redeemer lives, and He shall stand at last on the earth; and after my skin is destroyed, this I know, that in my flesh I shall see God, whom I shall see for myself, and my eyes shall behold, and not another. How my heart yearns within me!* (Job 19:25–27 NKJV)

Through his experience, Job comes to understand in a new way the greatness and power of the Lord. As God directs, he prays for the friends who have criticized him, and God gives him twice as much as he lost. Praise enabled Job to persevere through his hardships, and it was a major factor in his ultimate restoration.

I call the praise that Job demonstrated "fiery furnace" praise. When you reach this dimension of praise, your praise is indestructible. After King Nebuchadnezzar threatened Shadrach, Meshach, and Abednego with the fiery furnace, they replied,

> *If it be so, our God whom we serve is able to deliver us from the burning fiery furnace, and he will deliver us out of thine hand, O king.* **But if not**, *be it known unto thee, O king, that we will not serve thy gods, nor worship the golden image which thou hast set up.*
> (Daniel 3:17–18, emphasis added)

They had an "if He does, and if He doesn't" praise: If God moves on our behalf, that's okay, but if He doesn't, He's still our God. Everything the enemy sends you is designed to steal the praise that you have built through your knowledge and experience of the Father. Yet a child of God who has a no-matter-what praise is standing in a place of power. This is why, whenever I feel disappointment coming, I say, "If He does or if He doesn't, I'm still all right."

The enemy wants to give us the impression that he is more powerful than God is. When God shows you something in His Word about your healing and deliverance, the enemy will quickly tell you that it isn't going to happen. You can tell him, "Nothing that you say will change my relationship with the One who made the promise."

> "If He does or if He doesn't, I'm still all right."

Encouraging Ourselves in the Lord Our God

Like Job, David experienced an attack of total destruction that threatened to overwhelm him. When David was fleeing from Saul, he and his men and their families took refuge in a Philistine town called Ziklag. It was a place of provision, rest, and security for them while David was waiting for God to show him the next step in his life. While David and his men were away, the Amalekites invaded, kidnapping the men's wives and children and burning the city to the ground. The Bible says that when David and his troops returned and discovered the devastation, they wept until they had no more strength to weep. Then the men whom David had led and loved threatened to stone him because they were beside themselves with grief.

David was *"greatly distressed"* (1 Samuel 30:6). It would have been easy for him to have been caught up in this vortex of destruction and sorrow. Instead, he *"encouraged himself in the LORD his God"* (v. 6). Perhaps he began to think of all the battles that he had won with God's strength. Maybe he remembered the faithfulness of God in preserving his life from Saul. David had been in the shadow of adversity and defeat before, and he understood that praise is part of the process of deliverance. It was David who said, *"Because he is at my right hand, I shall not be moved"* (Psalm 16:8), and *"The LORD is my light and my salvation; whom shall I fear? the LORD is the strength of my life; of whom shall I be afraid?"* (Psalm 27:1).

Before David asked the Lord if he should go after the Amalekites, I think he remembered that *"the steps of a good man are ordered by the LORD: and he delighteth in his way. Though he fall, he shall not be utterly cast down: for the LORD upholdeth him with his hand"* (Psalm 37:23–24). God told David that he would win and recover everything. He did as the Lord said, and he and his men reclaimed all the families and all the wealth that had been taken from Ziklag. David had encouraged himself with praise by acknowledging the power and goodness of God. Praise lifted him past his problem and removed the scars of this difficult experience.

Perhaps you are in a Job or Ziklag experience—one where all the blessings of God seem to have slipped away, where it seems that the enemy has finally defeated you and taken away everything that you value. Friends whom you have loved, helped, and encouraged have suddenly turned on you. No one believes in what you're doing anymore. It is a time of questioning if you have heard the voice of God correctly. You feel as Jesus did in the garden of Gethsamane: *"O my Father, if it be possible, let this cup pass from me: nevertheless not as I will, but as thou wilt"* (Matthew 26:39).

What do you do? You cry, you pray, and then you decide to stand. When we get under stress, we often revert back to old patterns of thinking and want to give up, but the new you is a person of faith. You always have a choice in a Job or Ziklag experience: Are you going to remember the goodness and faithfulness of God, or are you going to sink into depression and give up? These are the times when you need to stir up your faith, restore your expectation, and resurrect your praise.

The Horizon of Promise

When life has wounded us deeply, leaving scars that only God can remove, praise is a part of God's process of our healing. Deliverance is often filled with challenges and setbacks. Emotional and spiritual growth comes with difficulty. The Spirit of God seeks to renew our minds, while defeat, discouragement, and despair wage war for control. Sometimes, like Job and David, we suffer the loss of almost everything that is important to us. The only thing that we really "own" during these times is the ability to give God praise—but that praise is vital because it will enable us to hold on to our visions of healing and deliverance.

We must continually enter into the cycle of praise. Praise based on God's character and Word fuels our faith. This leads to a renewed expectation of the fulfillment of His promise, which resurrects patient and joyful praise in anticipation of His answer. The horizon of promise reappears as we exercise a working faith and enter into God's infinite realm of possibility.

Chapter Nine

"According to Your Faith"

Real faith is developed during times of testing and enables us to stay strong while God delivers us from our scars.

I met John during a very challenging period in his life. We were both attending a conference in Phoenix, Arizona, on the topic of improving effectiveness in ministry. Brochures for conferences come to me in the mail all the time from places that I have never heard of. Although I often throw them away, a few somehow become difficult to dispose of. That was the case with this conference. Each time I attempted to file the brochure under "No Way," I would put it back on my desk.

I am not sure whether it was a desire to go to Phoenix combined the will of God or just the will of God, but I made it to Arizona. I'm a person who generally enjoys the heat, but it was *hot* there. After registration, I was ushered with the other attendees into the main auditorium, which looked more like a theater than a church. Ironically, the room was the coldest I had ever been in. (In Arizona, air conditioning is apparently an advanced science.) I noticed that everyone there was making an effort to appear casual. It looked like a floral shirt convention, with people's first names printed in huge letters on their name tags.

Everyone was circling the room looking for a comfortable place to settle. I ended up sitting next to John. We exchanged the usual information: state, ministry size, and years in that position. He asked me what I had been preaching about recently. I told him that I had been speaking on Job and the testimony of his faith. As the seminar instructor began his talk, John asked to speak to me during the break.

People come to seminars for a variety of reasons. Some come to escape the challenges of ministry for a few days and to get some rest and refreshment, while others come with a more desperate agenda: they are looking for a revelation that will give them the strength to continue on in their lives or ministries. John was looking for a revelation.

When Our Faith Is Shaken

John had been a man of apparently great faith while experiencing the normal challenges of life and ministry. Always victorious and encouraging others in their faith, he was sure that he could believe God for any situation. Yet, when I met him, he was in the midst of an extremely difficult challenge. It was as if his name had been changed to Job. Both his parents and his brother had died tragically in the previous twelve months. He was shaken and did not know if his faith would take him through this period in his life. John felt totally betrayed by God. Intellectually, he knew that he hadn't been, but emotionally, it *felt* that way.

I didn't tell him that I knew how he was feeling because I had never gone through a similar situation. However, I told him what I had learned from my own experiences as well as the experiences of others who have gone through painful times: When we have been deeply hurt, we often feel as if our faith has fled from us. I then assured him that the God who had been there for him in lesser difficulties was the same God who would see him through these tragic circumstances.

I helped him to understand that, along with faith and God's anointing on our lives, we can also expect to go through tough times. Jesus said, *"In the world ye shall have tribulation: but be of good cheer; I have overcome the world"* (John 16:33), and Paul wrote, *"All that will live godly in Christ Jesus shall suffer persecution"* (2 Timothy 3:12). We can't choose the times, the circumstances, or the weights of our tests and trials, but we can know that God promises to be with us and to sustain us during them. Jesus will walk with us in the fire so that we won't become scarred by these experiences, but will overcome them and fulfill the purposes of God for our lives:

> When we have been deeply hurt, we often feel as if our faith has fled from us.

> *Though now for a season, if need be, ye are in heaviness through manifold temptations: that the trial of your faith, being much more precious than of gold that perisheth, though it be tried with fire, might be found unto praise and honour and glory at the appearing of Jesus Christ.*
>
> (1 Peter 1:6–7)

Last, I told him that God allows us to carry only what we have the strength to bear. (See 1 Corinthians 10:13.) The weight of our burdens is always tipping us toward God's purposes for us. We are stumbling, but we are stumbling forward. We are tripping, but we are moving ahead. We are falling under the weight, but we are always falling forward so that we are farther along than we were. The weight presses us in the direction of isolation, vulnerability, rejection, and crucifixion. Yet crucifixion (surrendering ourselves to God's will) ultimately shows us the next steps to our destinies.

When we get to the place of crucifixion, we discover others who have been carrying their own personal burdens, yet have ended up in the same place of surrender, strengthened faith, and renewed purposes. As Paul wrote, *"I am crucified with Christ: nevertheless I live; yet not I, but Christ liveth in me: and the life which I now live in the flesh I live by the faith of the Son of God, who loved me, and gave himself for me"* (Galatians 2:20).

The reason we feel alone beneath these burdens is that no one else can carry them for us. The Bible says, *"Bear ye one another's burdens, and so fulfil the law of Christ"* (Galatians 6:2), but it also says, *"Every man shall bear his own burden"* (v. 5). We all have burdens that must be carried alone. There are some burdens that others may want to bear for us that we have to carry. These burdens break us of ourselves so that we may be rebuilt in Christ. They stretch us, but eventually stabilize us. They are painful, but they produce heartfelt praise to God. They may cause tears, but they always lead us to triumph. Our heavy weights lead us to new dimensions of strength in God.

> **Our burdens lead us to new dimensions of strength in God.**

When I explained all this to John, tears of release overflowed from his eyes. Neither of us minded who saw them. The *"eyes of* [his] *understanding"* (Ephesians 1:18) had been opened. He had gained a vision for God's purposes and for the way the Father desired to work in his life. He said that the heaviness had been lifted from him, and I could see that the dark cloud of his experience had gone. The hand of his faith had grasped the hand of encouragement that I had offered him; he was raised to a place where he could see himself as God saw him, and he was instantly healed of his hurt. Now that John's vision and faith had been resurrected, he would need to live out the process of complete deliverance from the scars that he had suffered, in the manner that I had just described to him.

The Process of Deliverance

Healing may come instantly, but being delivered from our scars is usually a process that requires persistent faith. In chapter 7, "Are You Ready to Say Yes?" we began to look at the role of faith in the fulfillment of God's vision for our lives. In the next two chapters, we will look at key facets of faith in regard to receiving our full deliverance and preventing additional wounds and scars. In this chapter, we will explore the faith that perseveres through tough times and periods of testing. In the next chapter, we will see how faith enables us to overcome the "impossible" situations of life.

God Is a Rewarder of Faith

Why is faith a key component in God's process of healing you and removing your scars? *"But without faith it is impossible to please him: for he that cometh to God must believe that he is, and that he is a rewarder of them that diligently seek him"* (Hebrews 11:6). God is a rewarder of faith. The Bible says that we must ask with faith that does not waver but trusts in God's faithfulness. *"Let us hold fast the profession of our faith without wavering; (for he is faithful that promised)"* (Hebrews 10:23). *"But let him ask in faith, nothing wavering. For he that wavereth is like a wave of the sea driven with the wind and tossed"* (James 1:6).

Faith is not a feeling, and it is not just a cerebral acknowl-edgment of a biblical fact. Faith *believes* and *trusts.* Believing is especially evident when we are obedient to the Word of God in times of trial and testing. Hebrews

Faith acts as if something is, even when it is not, in order that it might be.

10:36 says, *"You need to persevere so that when you have done the will of God, you will receive what he has promised"* (NIV). Faith acts as if something is so, even when it is not so, in order that it might be so. *"Now faith is the substance of things hoped for, the evidence of things not seen"* (Hebrews 11:1).

A Working Faith

Real faith is a working faith that reveals itself during adversity and stays strong while God heals us of our scars. God is a rewarder of those who diligently seek Him, by faith, in times of trouble. During these difficult times, your faith may waver, but it does not have to die. If you will allow them to, your troubles will serve to strengthen your faith so that you will become steadier each time you go through trials. You must continue to pray fervent prayers, knocking and believ-ing, until your wavering faith becomes strong faith.

The Bible declares that *"faith without works* [action] *is dead"* (James 2:20, 26). Jesus healed a blind man named Bartimaeus, who cast *"away his garment, rose, and came to Jesus"* (Mark 10:50) when the Lord called him. I see a symbol of deliverance in the man's act of casting aside his garment. If he had not left behind not only the garment of his past, but also the beggar's life that it represented, then his faith would have been dead. He might have received his sight without a vision of his com-plete deliverance. For him to have continued begging after receiving his sight would have been contrary to the will of God. Likewise, we need to go on to deliverance after receiving a vision of God's purposes for us as well as the healing of our wounds.

Jesus asked two other blind men, *"Believe ye that I am able to do this?"* (Matthew 9:28) because faith connects us with healing. *"Then touched he their eyes, saying, According to your faith be it unto you"* (v. 29). Faith is an invisible but vital link to the power of God. Without faith, healing and deliverance are impossible.

Admitting Our Weakness of Faith

Many people have difficulty admitting when their faith is weak. Instead, they celebrate their faith after the victory, conveniently leaving their temporary loss of faith during the fight out of their testimonies. I think that their testimonies would have greater effect if their hearers understood that their victories required enduring a wound here and there. Likewise, I believe that the greater testimony is not about walking on the water, but about

> We are never to step out on the water; we are to step out on Jesus' command concerning the water.

calling and reaching for Jesus by faith when you begin to sink, and Him saving you. It is God's Word, not our own faith, that we are to trust in. We are never to step out on the water; we are to step out on Jesus' command concerning the water, as He says to us, *"Come"* (Matthew 14:29). Faith tells me that, if I am in a storm, walking on top of a situation through the Word, then the Word will lift me if I start to sink and am in need of help.

We need to learn to develop our faith rather than pretend that it is strong when it is not. Just like John in the story that opened this chapter, we tend to evaluate the strength of our faith in good times, only to find that the strength of that faith is theoretical rather than experiential. For many of us, faith is often more of a feeling than a reality. It is the testing and wounding situations of life that expose the true dimensions of our belief. The challenge of faith is this: You don't know how much faith you have until you need it. All of us have been surprised and disappointed when our faith in good times is revealed to be completely different from our faith in difficult times.

Negative experiences can drain faith, virtue, and strength from us, but we are often unaware of these losses when they occur. For example, prizefighters don't always know the fatiguing or injurious effects of a previous fight until they are in the heat of a new battle. A similar thing happens to people of faith: The draining effects of previous tests and trials can go unnoticed until similar situations arise that reveal them.

> We need to learn to develop our faith rather than pretend it is strong when it is not.

An illustration of this principle is the impact that negative relationships can have on those involved. Often, a shattered relationship can alter your ability to cope well in a new relationship. The hurt that you've experienced can reduce your tolerance for dealing with the normal stresses of life—leaving you insecure, untrusting, and short-tempered, and leaving the other person hurt and bewildered. In these circumstances, many people take refuge in silence, but this only further sabotages their ability to communicate with the people in their new relationships.

I've found that the anger that we currently experience is often tied to unresolved issues in our pasts, which causes us to overreact to present situations. We begin to take out on the present person the anger that should have been expressed in the previous relationship. The result is relationship disability. Again, the disability is often not revealed until we enter a new relationship and sense that something that we had earlier is now missing. The natural thing to do is to force ourselves to believe that all is well with us, while blaming the other person for the problem. It is easier to shift blame than it is to work at healing the wound.

Again, we are not totally aware of our ability to handle the difficulties of life until we actually experience tough times. Very little faith is needed when there is no struggle. God uses our struggles to build our faith, but most people don't realize this, and therefore they try to avoid difficulties. Yet, as true ability is proven under pressure, real faith is developed in times of adversity.

> **Very little faith is needed when there is no struggle.**

The Triumph of Faith

Hebrews 11 is a testimony to those who were diligent in faith during difficult circumstances and times of testing, and of God's faithfulness to them. Let's look at some of the men and women featured in this chapter.

The Faith of Abraham and Sarah

By faith Abraham obeyed when he was called to go out to the place which he would receive as an inheritance. And he went out, not knowing where he was going. By faith he dwelt

in the land of promise as in a foreign country, dwelling in tents with Isaac and Jacob, the heirs with him of the same promise; for he waited for the city which has foundations, whose builder and maker is God. By faith Sarah herself also received strength to conceive seed, and she bore a child when she was past the age, because she judged Him faithful who had promised. Therefore from one man, and him as good as dead, were born as many as the stars of the sky in multitude; innumerable as the sand which is by the seashore....By faith Abraham, when he was tested, offered up Isaac, and he who had received the promises offered up his only begotten son, of whom it was said, "In Isaac your seed shall be called," concluding that God was able to raise him up, even from the dead, from which he also received him in a figurative sense.
(Hebrews 11:8–12, 17–19 NKJV)

Abraham needed faith to believe God's word concerning the Promised Land, which he had never seen and which could be reached only through isolation and loneliness. Then, he and Sarah had to have faith for the birth of their miracle son, Isaac, whom they could receive only after going through years of personal disappointment. Through his belief in God, Abraham became the father of the faith and received a declaration of righteousness from God. Later, Abraham needed faith that God could raise the dead when he was tested by God and told to sacrifice his child of promise. His willingness to obey God brought him even more favor with the Lord, who acknowledged Abraham's complete faithfulness, saying, *"Lay not thine hand upon the lad, neither do thou any thing unto him: for now I know that thou fearest God, seeing thou hast not withheld thy son, thine only son from me"* (Genesis 22:12). God provided a ram as a sacrifice instead of Isaac, and restored Abraham's son to him.

The Faith of Joseph

"By faith Joseph, when he was dying, made mention of the departure of the children of Israel, and gave instructions concerning his bones" (Hebrews 11:22 NKJV). Joseph depended upon his faith in God to sustain him after his dreams of destiny looked as if they would never be fulfilled. He dreamed that he would become a ruler, but he initially experienced the complete opposite of this when he became a slave. He needed a persistent faith to endure the rebuke of his father, the hatred and betrayal of his brothers, the pit of isolation, the slavery of Potiphar's house, the temptation of Potiphar's wife, and the prison where he was apparently forgotten. The Bible says that, through all these experiences, *"the LORD was with Joseph"* (Genesis 39:2, 21), and he eventually became a great ruler in fulfillment of God's vision for his life. Finally, when it was time for him to die, Joseph exercised faith that God would continue to be with his family's descendants, the children of Israel, in fulfillment of His promise to Abraham. He made sure that, when they left Egypt, they would carry his remains into the Promised Land with them. (See Genesis 37, 39–50.)

The Faith of Moses

By faith Moses, when he was born, was hidden three months by his parents, because they saw he was a beautiful child; and they were not afraid of the king's command. By faith Moses, when he became of age, refused to be called the son of Pharaoh's daughter, choosing rather to suffer affliction with the people of God than to enjoy the passing pleasures of sin, esteeming the reproach of Christ greater riches than the treasures in Egypt; for he looked to the reward. By faith he forsook Egypt, not fearing the wrath of the king; for he

endured as seeing Him who is invisible....By faith they passed through the Red Sea as by dry land, whereas the Egyptians, attempting to do so, were drowned.
(Hebrews 11:23–27, 29 NKJV)

Moses had to have faith to accomplish all that God had called him to do because leading God's people out of Egypt was not an easy task—or one that came naturally to him. First, he was a Hebrew who was raised by a surrogate Egyptian family to be someone that he was never destined to be. Second, he became a fugitive, disconnected from his homeland and living among strangers. Third, he received an extraordinary message of destiny from God through a burning bush that no one else heard or saw. Fourth, he was sent to confront the Pharaoh of Egypt, the most powerful ruler in the world at that time. Fifth, he was called to lead the Hebrew multitude safely out of Egyptian slavery and into the wilderness so that they could enter the Promised Land. In the midst of all these things, Moses had to overcome self-doubt and low self-esteem. (See Exodus 1–14.)

The Faith of Rahab

"By faith the walls of Jericho fell down after they were encircled for seven days. By faith the harlot Rahab did not perish with those who did not believe, when she had received the spies with peace" (Hebrews 11:30–31 NKJV). Rahab needed faith to overcome her negative origins as a prostitute among a people who did not know the Lord, and a potentially hopeless future of being captured or killed when the Israelites invaded her city. When the Israelite spies, under Joshua's direction, came to scope out Jericho, she counted herself among God's people. She helped the spies to escape detection, asking them to spare her life

and the lives of her family members during the assault. Her covenant with the God of Israel through Joshua would not only save her and her household, but also deliver her from her own personal Jericho, a self-destructive lifestyle. The Bible tells us that Rahab became the mother of Boaz, who was the husband of Ruth, and that she was the great-grandmother of King David, from whom Jesus Christ was descended. (See Matthew 1:5–6.)

Faith Comes by Hearing

These men and women of faith moved through their testing and trials and emerged from them without scars. We, also, need to exercise an active faith. God never leaves us without resources to understand and do His will. He will provide the vision for our healing and deliverance, on which we can base our faith. Remember that what the blind men's eyes could not behold, their ears received. They didn't see Jesus, but they heard His voice and responded in faith. (See Matthew 9:28–29.) The Bible doesn't say that faith is a product of seeing; it says that *faith cometh by hearing*" (Romans 10:17).

> God has a word that is tailor-made for your situation.

Whenever Jesus spoke in parables, He usually ended with, *"He that hath ears to hear, let him hear."* (See, for example, Matthew 13:9, Mark 4:9, Luke 14:35.) The blind men's response to what they heard connected them to their healing. It began when they received Jesus' word for their situation, which prepared them to receive their restoration through faith. God has a word that is tailor-made for your situation. It may be a word that you have read before but that takes on new meaning for you through the power of the Holy Spirit. The Word of God

171

connects you to His will and impregnates you with power, purpose, and destiny.

Faith Is a Gift That Must Be Developed

The Bible says that faith is a gift that we receive: *"God has dealt to each one a measure of faith"* (Romans 12:3 NKJV). It also says that we must develop our gift. Paul indicated this truth to the early believers: *"Our hope is that, as your faith continues to grow, our area of activity among you will greatly expand"* (2 Corinthians 10:15 NIV). *"Night and day praying exceedingly that we might…perfect that which is lacking in your faith"* (1 Thessalonians 3:10). *"We are bound to thank God always for you, brethren, as it is fitting, because your faith grows exceedingly"* (2 Thessalonians 1:3 NKJV).

Faith Can Become a Natural Reaction to Life's Challenges

If our negative circumstances reveal a loss or lack of faith in our lives, we must not hide from this reality but instead address it and learn how to grow in our faith. A child of God without working faith is like a bird with wings that refuses to fly. Flight is a necessity for a bird's survival. It gives the bird access to the dimensions that it has been empowered to reach. Flight moves a bird from places of need to places of supply, from danger to safety, and from unfavorable environments to favorable environments.

All birds must learn to fly. They begin tentatively at first. Then, with increased strength and faith in their gift, flight becomes to them a natural reaction to the challenges they encounter. They have been gifted by God to maximize the ability that they were created to exercise. It is the same with the child of God. Faith is your God-given ability to fly. It allows you to reach the mental, emotional, and spiritual dimensions that you were meant for.

Faith, like flight, equips you to handle the challenges of life. It moves you from insufficiency to sufficiency, from lack to plenty, from danger to safety, from dishonor to honor, from wounds to health, and from scars to deliverance. God has given you faith to rise above all the challenges of life. With practice, it will become your natural reaction to testing and trial.

> Faith is your God-given ability to fly.

"The trying of your faith worketh patience" (James 1:3). The testing of your faith prepares you for the day when strong faith is needed. The fire of your challenges refines, purifies, and prepares your faith for greater possibilities in the future.

Faith Transforms Tribulations

Romans 5:1–4 says,

Therefore being justified by faith, we have peace with God through our Lord Jesus Christ: by whom also we have access by faith into this grace wherein we stand, and rejoice in hope of the glory of God. And not only so, but we glory in tribulations also: knowing that tribulation worketh patience; and patience, experience [trustworthiness]; *and experience* [trustworthiness], *hope.*

The moment that you are saved by faith, God declares that you are righteous. In that declaration is the promise of the peace of God, access into His grace, and personal growth and transformation during tribulations.

Peace comes from knowing and experiencing the will of God through faith. In spite of the wounds that you have received and the scars that have developed as a result, you have been positioned to experience peace that goes beyond our everyday definition of the word. God's peace *"surpasses all understanding"* (Philippians 4:7 NKJV) and is not dependant on circumstances.

Our faithful God teaches us that adversity is not meant to be destructive in our lives, but instructive. Difficulty is a faith-strengthening, fruit-producing part of His will and promise concerning you. You must experience adversity to fully appreciate God's peace and grace.

Paul called adversity *"tribulation."* No one likes problems, and most people avoid trouble at all costs. Unfortunately, trouble has a way of finding us. Yet the Bible assures us that, when we are living in the grace and power of God, trouble will ultimately build us up instead of tearing us down. In God's protective custody, trouble *"worketh"* some important things in our lives, such as patience, trustworthiness, and hope for the future.

> Peace comes from knowing and experiencing the will of God through faith.

The word *"worketh"* in the original Greek means "to work fully, i.e. accomplish; by implication to finish, fashion." (See *Strong's,* #G2716.) Satan's mission is to kill your faith, steal your hope, and destroy your destiny. Yet, in Christ, the very adversity that Satan wants to use to destroy you is transformed into a refining and maturing experience. This experience ultimately produces more faith as God works all things for your good. *"And we know that all things work together for good to them that love God, to them who are the called according to his purpose"* (Romans 8:28).

Instead of allowing trouble to drive us crazy, we can live in peace and learn patience. While we are learning patience, our trustworthiness can be built. As our trustworthiness is built, our hope can be secured. All these benefits begin with the challenges of life that, at first, seem designed to limit our possibilities.

Faith Helps Us to Accept God's Timing

One of the reasons that we need to develop patience is that God's timing is usually very different from ours. His timing tests the integrity of our faith. We often misunderstand God because, when negative things occur, we can get the impression that He is not paying attention to our needs. Yet having a relationship with God does not guarantee that painful situations will never occur. When unpleasant things happen, we must remember that the Lord will still bring healing and deliverance. *"But unto you that fear my name shall the Sun of righteousness arise with healing in his wings"* (Malachi 4:2).

Our response to our trials during this time of waiting indicates to God what we truly believe about Him. Our faith often wavers when what we see causes us to be double-minded about what we believe. God allows us to go through tests and trials so we will finally realize that, just because we *feel* as if we can't take our difficulties any longer, that doesn't mean that our faith can't actually bear them. We usually connect our faith to our physical, mental, or emotional ability to take the stress that we are facing, but again, God would never release something in our lives that He didn't know that we had the faith to handle. (See 1 Corinthians 10:13.) Once we understand that it's not God's mission to defeat us, but to strengthen us, we begin to look at our situations differently because we know that we can overcome them in Him.

Faith rises above knowledge and emotion. Paul said, *"Your faith should not be in the wisdom of men but in the power of God"* (1 Corinthians 2:5 NKJV). Even when we give up on a situation in our hearts, our faith can continue to operate. I may not have faith in me, but I have faith in God. I have found that, sometimes, if we get down low enough, we will believe God for things that we have never believed Him for before.

> Faith rises above knowledge and emotion.

Perception versus Faith

One of the great hindrances to faith is perception—the way we perceive the strength of our problems compared to the way we perceive the power of God. We shift between belief based on what we are seeing and experiencing versus our faith in Him. Often, we begin to believe in the problem more than we believe in God because the problem is right in front of us, while we don't yet see His provision. This is when we need a true vision of God's power and faithfulness.

Often, we can be swayed by the perceptions of others who don't think that our healing and deliverance is possible. When Jesus healed the blind men, it was because they had caught His vision for their lives, even though the crowd had not. The two men shared the same dream, and they agreed on the outcome. We need partners in faith who understand not only the nature of the problem, but also the nature of God. Jesus told the blind men, *"According to your faith be it unto you"* (Matthew 9:29).

Promises Reserved in Heaven

The book of Acts tells us that the works of God were known to Him before the world began. (See Acts 15:18.) Everything that God has promised us was complete in Him before the beginning of time. The blind men had a healing in heaven reserved for them that was waiting for their faith to release it from eternity in their time of need. Faith brings the power of God from heaven to earth. Jesus said, *"Thy kingdom come. Thy will be done in earth, as it is in heaven"* (Matthew 6:10).

There is power reserved for you for the healing of your wounds and the removal of the scars in your life. This power produces long-term deliverance and prevents recurring wounds and pain. Our passion for the promises of God can begin to evaporate while we're waiting for His timing. Yet we can draw on His power and Word to enable us to persevere until we see the fulfillment of the promises, just as Abraham, Sarah, Joseph, Moses, Rahab, and multitudes of other believers have. *"And we desire that each one of you show the same diligence to the full assurance of hope until the end, that you do not become sluggish, but imitate those who through faith and patience inherit the promises"* (Hebrews 6:11–12 NKJV).

Chapter Ten

The Infinite Realm
of Possibility

True deliverance is our being changed in the midst of a situation before the situation changes.

When I met Mark, he felt hopeless. I was leading a Sunday night deliverance service when I spotted him in the congregation. Throughout the entire evening, his face was very evident to me in the crowd. He looked lost—too lost for a young man his age.

Mark had tried to kill himself several times, and was still suicidal. He had given up hope that his mind would ever be normal and that his emotions would ever stabilize. He had been feeling this way for so long and acting out so severely that his family had given up on him. His behavior had become increasingly more destructive, yet his destructiveness was a cry for an end to the torment that he felt no one else really understood.

An Act of Desperation

Time and again, Mark had tried to express what he felt to his family, friends, and doctors. No one seemed able to help. They offered advice, compassion, pity, and support, but they could not reach the source of his condition.

Mark believed in God and had been exposed to church, but he had no relationship with either. The night that he came to the service at my church, he had been drinking. He had seen the cars in the parking lot of the church and, in an act of desperation, had come inside. It was to be his last stop before ending his life. He believed that his life was void of all positive possibility.

At the end of the service, I called for prayer, and many people moved toward the altar. Desperation will drive you to do some things that you've never done before, and Mark came up for prayer. As I reached his place in the prayer line, I realized that his need and desperation had positioned him to receive from God. However, he could not clearly articulate his problem or tell me what he wanted for himself out of life. What I did understand was that he had a very difficult relationship with his father.

As I began to talk to Mark, I realized that the length of his suffering and his loss of hope were deafening him to my words. I stopped talking to him and instead spoke to his pain, the dysfunction in his home, his combative relationship with his father, and his personal failure. I spoke to his substance abuse, which was his attempt to cover his pain.

A Reason to Live

Mark felt that he had no reason to live, but he did have a reason—God's love for him and His purposes for his life. All he needed was the validation of the Father. I began to pray for insight and then prayed for the words to say. I told him what it was like for me to grow up in the presence of a violent, alcoholic father. Then I told Mark that his own father was trying to make him as miserable as he was. Often, when parents are unhappy, all they are capable of doing is transferring that loss of purpose to their children. It is a twisted way to guarantee transference of legacy, no matter how dysfunctional that heritage is. It is a warped way of reproducing yourself, positioning the next generation for the same pain, wounding, and scarring.

Mark felt as if he was being torn in two. Part of him wanted to escape his relationship with his father, while the other part wanted to stay connected. I told Mark that he did not have to become his father. I spoke to his misguided desire to emulate his father as a show of loyalty. In a sense, Mark had been willing to die to show his father how badly he desired his affirmation and attention. I told him that Christ had already died for both him and his father. He did not have to die for his father's sake; that was a sacrifice he wasn't required to make. The saying is true: Suicide is a permanent solution to a temporary problem. His death would only rob God of the opportunity to bless him.

True Deliverance Is Our Being Changed

Mark's breakthrough began. His drunken state suddenly cleared, and his eyes, speech, and balance stabilized. The anointing of God on him was tangibly present. I told him that he was not allowed to die, that God had a purpose for his life. He realized, despite his experiences, that his life was not over. I asked him if he was ready to receive Jesus as his Savior, making Him the Lord of his life. He was ready. As I reached out and embraced him, he fell into me as though he had been waiting for this for a long time. He began to sob as though pain were being released with every breath. He had a loving Father now. He had experienced the Father's touch and could receive God's promise and purpose for his life.

I cautioned Mark about what he would face during the next few days: Satan would challenge every component of his deliverance. He would be dealing with the same earthly father, and he would be living in the same home. His friends would remain the same. The key was that *he* had changed. True deliverance is our being changed in the midst of a situation before the situation changes. The same challenges would remain, but Mark never needed to respond to them the same again. God had given him strength to rise above his surroundings and to begin to experience all the possibilities in life. The Father had preserved him for his future.

> **Satan will challenge every component of your deliverance.**

When Old Methods No Longer Work

Perhaps you feel as if your emotions, self-esteem, confidence, faith, joy, and sense of peace will never receive healing. You can exist in a scarred mind-set for so long that what is abnormal seems normal to you. Maybe some of the conditions that you've been dealing with have lasted for so long that they seem to have been with you for your entire life. To survive emotionally, you no longer want to hope that they will ever go away. You believe that you will never feel any differently.

Or perhaps you are confronting a situation in which your prayers don't appear to be making any difference. The methods of the past suddenly seem to reveal themselves as shallow. You fall back on habit, but the old solutions just don't work. The person you thought you were is not equipped for the trials of the present. The voice of God seems distant, while the presence of God seems adversarial.

I remember going through a particularly rough time in my life when this was the case. Before that season, I was sure that I had mountain-moving faith. Then a mountain appeared that did not move in response to my prayers. I praised God, but it did not move. I fasted and was anointed with oil, but the mountain defiantly continued to exist. With each apparent spiritual failure, my faith took a hit. This was because I was placing my hopes in my ability to have faith, when what I needed was faith in God's ability to move the mountain. As I wrote earlier, faith in our faith is limited to our capacity to handle the negative situation. My faith in my faith was connected to my strength, not God's, and I became weary. I was still anointed by God to serve and encourage others, but the faith that I had for other people did not seem to work for me.

> **What I needed was faith in God's ability to move the mountain.**

During this time, I learned something about myself: It was easier for me to have faith for another person's circumstance than for my own—even if the problems were very similar. The application of my faith for others' incarcerated children, marital difficulties, unemployment problems, or depression is what I call an "objectively empathetic" faith. I am empathetic because we share common problems, but my association with these situations lacks emotion and connectedness. Unlike Christ, who is *"touched with the feeling of our infirmities"* (Hebrews 4:15), I can know what it's like to go through what you have been through, but I don't know what it's like to *be* you.

Also, if my faith fails for these situations, the personal impact is not nearly as great as if I were directly involved. My faith for others takes little emotional investment. Sympathy and empathy cost nothing. It is personal participation in a situation that takes an emotional toll. It's not really the problem that affects my faith—it's how I *feel* about the problem that causes my faith to waver.

Against Overwhelming Odds

I guarantee you that your faith will be challenged. Your enemy, Satan, seeks to steal your hope, kill your dreams, and destroy your access to the unlimited possibilities of God. He begins his attack as early in your life as possible so that the wounds of your youth and the scars that develop will defer or defeat God's purposes for you.

When the odds seem overwhelming, our situations can threaten to obscure God's personal revelation for us. What do we do when our circumstances seem hopeless and our "normal" way of living, praying, and believing doesn't seem to be effective? It is imperative, at these times, that our journey is a walk of faith and not circumstantially driven. Our faith has to reach past the wounds and scars and lay hold of the healing and delivering power of the infinite realm of possibility in God.

What is your secret petition to God? You think it sounds crazy because circumstances make it seem as if it's never going to happen. There are things in my own life that I despair over at times. I wonder if God is ever going to fix them. I now realize that the reason I wonder about them is that I can't make sense of *how* He's going to do it. Yet I have discovered that when we don't know what to say on our own behalf, our faith will cry out for us. Faith will grab an opportunity that we almost missed because we were blinded to the presence of God by our situations. Faith will seize the moment and kick down the door to a breakthrough.

> When we don't know what to say, our faith will cry out for us.

When There Seems to Be No Future

A number of people in the Bible faced impossible situations until they encountered the power of God through faith. Let's look at several of their stories. The first is about a boy with a lifelong problem that continually produced physical and emotional scars.

The Boy Who Was Demon-Possessed

And when [Jesus] came to his disciples, he saw a great multitude about them, and the scribes questioning with them. And straightway all the people, when they beheld him, were greatly amazed, and running to him saluted him. And he asked the scribes, What question ye with them? And one of the multitude answered and said, Master, I have brought unto thee my son, which hath a dumb spirit; and wheresoever he taketh him, he teareth him: and he foameth, and gnasheth with his teeth, and pineth away: and I spake to thy disciples that they should cast him out; and they could not. (Mark 9:14–18)

In this circumstance, the disciples appear powerless to help the boy, while the father seems resigned to his son's apparent limited potential. The son is described as having a *"dumb spirit."* He has a problem that he is unable to express but that reveals itself in destructive behavior. Likewise, we are often wounded and scarred so deeply that we cannot express the silent cry of our pain.

> [Jesus] *answereth him, and saith, O faithless generation, how long shall I be with you? how long shall I suffer you? bring him unto me. And they brought him unto him: and when he saw him, straightway the spirit tare him; and he fell on the ground, and wallowed foaming. And he asked his father, How long is it ago since this came unto him? And he said, Of a child. And ofttimes it hath cast him into the fire, and into the waters, to destroy him: but if thou canst do any thing, have compassion on us, and help us.* (vv. 19–22)

The father explains that his son has had this problem for most of his life. Imprisoned by his pain, bound to failure by his actions, the boy has watched others function normally while he has missed one opportunity after another. This *"spirit,"* this problem, wants to silence the voice of his future, limiting his opportunities and killing his possibilities. The boy is locked in frustration, wondering, "Will I ever feel any differently?"

When he is brought to the disciples for help, they are unable to cure him. The father asks Jesus, "Is there anything that You can do? Please have compassion on us and help us." The problem is no longer just the boy's. It seems that the feeling of his infirmity touches all those connected with him. They are suffering because they care deeply for him. His wounds and scars are testing the endurance of their love because they don't know if he will ever change. His problem has become so extreme that they are now afraid for his life.

Jesus said unto [the father], *If thou canst believe, all things are possible to him that believeth. And straightway the father of the child cried out, and said with tears, Lord, I believe; help thou mine unbelief.*   (vv. 23–24)

The father believes, but he is experiencing some unbelief. This unbelief is based on the duration and severity of his son's condition. Jesus tells him, *"If thou canst believe, all things are possible to him that believeth."* Jesus makes a profound, situation-altering statement. He assures this father, as well as all of us, that our possibilities are as limitless as our faith in God's nature and power. Faith is the key to the promises and the unlimited realm known as the kingdom of God. Entrance into this kingdom of promise is initiated through a saving relationship with Jesus. As He begins to live in us, our relationship with Him uniquely positions us to live in the dual reality of life, which we talked about earlier. There is the reality of the material world, but there is another reality in the realm of the Spirit—the kingdom of God. Faith takes us past a mere perception of the kingdom and into participation with the unlimited power of that kingdom.

When Jesus saw that the people came running together, he rebuked the foul spirit, saying unto him, Thou dumb and deaf spirit, I charge thee, come out of him, and enter no more into him. And the spirit cried, and rent him sore, and came out of him: and he was as one dead; insomuch that many said, He is dead. But Jesus took him by the hand, and lifted him up; and he arose. And when he was come into the house, his disciples asked him privately, Why could not we cast him out? And he said unto them, This kind can come forth by nothing, but by prayer and fasting.

(vv. 25–29)

There is no pain beyond Christ's ability to heal. No matter how long you have fought your inner battle with a real, silent enemy, you can receive the Father's touch. Jesus will speak to the source of your wounds and the reality of your scars, and bring you deliverance.

> There is no pain beyond Christ's ability to heal.

The Widow Who Lost Her Only Son

We meet the widow from Nain during a funeral procession for her only son. She is at a breaking point in her life. Often, at our breaking point, our vision for ourselves becomes blurred. We begin to question our faith, ability, and strength. I imagine that this is what it was like for the widow.

> [Jesus] *went into a city called Nain; and many of his disciples went with him, and much people. Now when he came nigh to the gate of the city, behold, there was a dead man carried out, the only son of his mother, and she was a widow: and much people of the city was with her. And when the Lord saw her, he had compassion on her, and said unto her, Weep not. And he came and touched the bier: and they that bare him stood still. And he said, Young man, I say unto thee, Arise. And he that was dead sat up, and began to speak. And he delivered him to his mother.* (Luke 7:11–15)

The woman's son represents her future, yet her provision and promise are headed for the cemetery. (In the times in which she lived, being a widow with no children means that she now has no visible means of support.) Her future potential, provision, and possibility appear lost. She believes that her future is out of her hands and that she has to bury her hopes for a meaningful and happy life. If the day of the funeral is overcast and dreary, she will remember it as a fitting backdrop for her sorrow and hopelessness. If the day sunny, she will forever remember it as a cruel paradox to her grief.

The day of the funeral seems so final, and she is not alone in her acceptance of it. Many people from her city are accompanying her to the grave site. Perhaps she is a well-known and well-regarded member of the community. In any event, these people have accepted her dilemma as a permanent part of her life's story. Maybe she wonders if any of them will extend charity to her as she faces the insecurity of relying on the kindness of others.

To me, the pallbearers carrying the coffin represent the fact that there are always those who are willing to help write off your future and bury your promise, while there are few who have the faith to help you restore it. In the woman's eyes and the eyes of the others, her realm of possibility is significantly limited. But Jesus is the Lord of possibility, and He is coming her way.

Jesus has been eternally on His way to interrupt the burial of her provision and promise. On His journey from glory to Calvary and back to glory, His life and power are destined to intersect with her impossibility. Jesus tells her not to weep, and then He touches the *"bier,"* or coffin, and stops the procession. He makes contact with the thing that holds her lost possibility. The coffin represents the loss of hope, promise, purpose, and strength in her life. It also represents her inability to effect a change in her situation, and her acceptance of her lost potential.

Jesus speaks to the apparent finality of the situation, saying, *"Young man, I say unto thee, Arise"* (Luke 7:14). The son sits up and begins to speak, and Jesus presents him to his mother. The funeral was an interruption of the young man's potential and his mother's future, not the end of them. When they encountered Jesus, they entered the infinite realm of possibility.

The Woman Who Sacrificed Out of Her Need

In the Old Testament, there is the story of another widow who loses all hope for herself and her son. After enduring the death of her husband, she faces two more impossible situations: starvation and the loss of her boy.

> *And it came to pass after a while, that the brook dried up, because there had been no rain in the land. And the word of the* LORD *came unto* [Elijah]*, saying, Arise, get thee to Zarephath, which belongeth to Zidon, and dwell there: behold, I have commanded a widow woman there to sustain thee. So he arose and went to Zarephath. And when he came to the gate of the city, behold, the widow woman was there gathering of sticks: and he called to her, and said, Fetch me, I pray thee, a little water in a vessel, that I may drink. And as she was going to fetch it, he called to her, and said, Bring me, I pray thee, a morsel of bread in thine hand. And she said, As the* LORD *thy God liveth, I have not a cake, but an handful of meal in a barrel, and a little oil in a cruse: and, behold, I am gathering two sticks, that I may go in and dress it for me and my son, that we may eat it, and die.* (1 Kings 17:7–12)

The prophet Elijah encounters the woman at the gate of the city. She is gathering sticks to make a fire for the final meal that she and her son will ever eat. He breaks the silence of her misery by asking her to bring him a drink of water and a little bread because he knows that God has promised to provide for his needs through her.

The requests force her to evaluate her possibilities. She has a little meal and oil for a cake, which is just enough for her son and herself, and she explains this dilemma to Elijah. Fear has become an issue in her life, and fear is often the adversary of obedience. Yet obedience, like faith, is a bridge to breakthrough.

> *And Elijah said unto her, Fear not; go and do as thou hast said: but make me thereof a little cake first, and bring it unto me, and after make for thee and for thy son. For thus saith the* Lord *God of Israel, The barrel of meal shall not waste, neither shall the cruse of oil fail, until the day that the* Lord *sendeth rain upon the earth. And she went and did according to the saying of Elijah: and she, and he, and her house, did eat many days. And the barrel of meal wasted not, neither did the cruse of oil fail, according to the word of the* Lord, *which he spake by Elijah.*   (vv. 13–16)

Through Elijah the prophet, God is asking this woman to give Him a sacrifice out of her need rather than her abundance. A sacrifice out of your need requires faith. Elijah doesn't ask her to exercise blind faith, however. He speaks a prophetic promise concerning the resurrection of her possibilities and the transformation of her situation. It is a word that honors her sacrifice while illustrating the restorative power of the anointing.

A sacrifice out of your need requires faith.

The Bible says that God's Word cannot fail; it will not return to Him void, but accomplish His purposes. (See Isaiah 55:11.) The woman needed a word for her situation that would reignite the passion of her faith and resurrect her confident hope. When she hears and obeys this word from God through

Elijah, her circumstances are transformed. Each time she exercises her faith in the word from God by dipping into the barrel of meal or pouring oil from the vessel, promise replenishes her supply.

The woman is living in the power of the anointing. It is interesting to note that the Bible no longer calls her a *"widow woman"* (1 Kings 17:9, 10). She is now referred to as *"the mistress of the house"* (v. 17), the one in charge. Through the power of God, she has become self-sufficient. She is able to feed her son, who represents her future promise and provision. She is also able to provide for Elijah, who is a guest at her house. Her situation has been changed by her revelation of what God desires to do in her life.

As often happens, however, when we are delivered in one area of our lives, another challenge occurs. In the woman's case, her son becomes ill and dies.

> *And it came to pass after these things, that the son of the woman, the mistress of the house, fell sick; and his sickness was so sore, that there was no breath left in him. And she said unto Elijah, What have I to do with thee, O thou man of God? art thou come unto me to call my sin to remembrance, and to slay my son?* (vv. 17–18)

After all that she has endured and the miraculous way that God has provided for her, her son dies. Like so many people before and after her who have experienced difficult times, the woman believes that God is playing a horrible trick on her. His death is not consistent with the revelation of provision that she has received.

> *And [Elijah] said unto her, Give me thy son. And he took him out of her bosom, and carried him up into a loft, where*

he abode, and laid him upon his own bed. And he cried unto the LORD, and said, O LORD my God, hast thou also brought evil upon the widow with whom I sojourn, by slaying her son? And he stretched himself upon the child three times, and cried unto the LORD, and said, O LORD my God, I pray thee, let this child's soul come into him again. And the LORD heard the voice of Elijah; and the soul of the child came into him again, and he revived. And Elijah took the child, and brought him down out of the chamber into the house, and delivered him unto his mother: and Elijah said, See, thy son liveth. (vv. 19–23)

When the woman cries out to Elijah for help, he simply says, "Give me your son." When we face similar dilemmas, we are to place them into the hands of Jesus and let Him take care of them. Remember that the Shunammite woman also released her promise, her miracle son, into the care of Elisha, illustrating what we are to do when hope dies. She gave her son to God, and He resurrected her possibility. (See 2 Kings 4:1–37.) In a similar way, Elijah prays for this woman's son, and the Lord hears his voice. The woman experiences the resurrection of her future possibilities in the restoration of her son, which brings wholeness to her life.

The Friend of Jesus Who Died

Now a certain man was sick, named Lazarus, of Bethany, the town of Mary and her sister Martha. (It was that Mary which anointed the Lord with ointment, and wiped his feet with her hair, whose brother Lazarus was sick.) Therefore his sisters sent unto him, saying, Lord, behold, he whom thou lovest is sick. When Jesus heard that, he said, This sickness is not unto death, but for the glory of God, that the Son of God might be glorified thereby. Now Jesus loved Martha, and her sister, and Lazarus. (John 11:1–5)

Lazarus was a special friend of Jesus, and other passages of Scripture indicate that he made room in his home for Jesus to stay whenever He came to town. I have the impression that Lazarus and his sisters, Mary and Martha, lived together in unity. The passage says that Jesus loved them. Despite the family's relationship, fellowship, worship, and service to Jesus, however, Lazarus became sick and died. His future was suddenly interrupted, and the leader and provider of the house was taken away. Again, we see women without husbands who are left with no visible means of support. All this happens while they are in close relationship with the Lord. We must remember that, even when we have a relationship with Jesus, things will, at times, appear to go out of control.

Then when Jesus came, he found that [Lazarus] *had lain in the grave four days already. Now Bethany was nigh unto Jerusalem, about fifteen furlongs off: and many of the Jews came to Martha and Mary, to comfort them concerning their brother. Then Martha, as soon as she heard that Jesus was coming, went and met him: but Mary sat still in the house. Then said Martha unto Jesus, Lord, if thou hadst been here, my brother had not died. But I know, that even now, whatsoever thou wilt ask of God, God will give it thee. Jesus saith unto her, Thy brother shall rise again. Martha saith unto him, I know that he shall rise again in the resurrection at the last day. Jesus said unto her, I am the resurrection, and the life: he that believeth in me, though he were dead, yet shall he live: and whosoever liveth and believeth in me shall never die. Believest thou this? She saith unto him,*

Yea, Lord: I believe that thou art the Christ, the Son of God, which should come into the world. (John 11:17–27)

Martha and Mary send for Jesus but, at first, He does not come. When He does arrive, He doesn't address their problem immediately. He simply tells Martha that the situation is not beyond His power. *"Thy brother shall arise again"* (v. 23). Then He asks Martha if she believes that He is the resurrection and the life. She believes, paving the way for the resurrection of her dead hopes. Likewise, your hope, promise, and potential will rise again as you trust the resurrection power of Jesus.

When Mary was come where Jesus was, and saw him, she fell down at his feet, saying unto him, Lord, if thou hadst been here, my brother had not died. When Jesus therefore saw her weeping, and the Jews also weeping which came with her, he groaned in the spirit, and was troubled, and said, Where have ye laid him? They said unto him, Lord, come and see. Jesus wept. (vv. 32–35)

Mary comes to Jesus in disappointment, but falls down at His feet in worship. It is the worshipper who brings Jesus to tears. A weeping worshipper always causes grace to overflow on the table of provision. Jesus asks, "Where have you laid him?" In other words, He was asking, "Show me where you have buried your hopes, dreams, and possibilities."

> A weeping worshipper always causes grace to overflow.

Jesus therefore again groaning in himself cometh to the grave. It was a cave, and a stone lay upon it. Jesus said, Take ye away the stone. Martha, the sister of him that was dead, saith unto him, Lord, by this time he stinketh: for he

195

hath been dead four days. Jesus saith unto her, Said I not unto thee, that, if thou wouldest believe, thou shouldest see the glory of God? Then they took away the stone from the place where the dead was laid. And Jesus lifted up his eyes, and said, Father, I thank thee that thou hast heard me. And I knew that thou hearest me always: but because of the people which stand by I said it, that they may believe that thou hast sent me. And when he thus had spoken, he cried with a loud voice, Lazarus, come forth. And he that was dead came forth, bound hand and foot with graveclothes: and his face was bound about with a napkin. Jesus saith unto them, Loose him, and let him go. (vv. 38–44)

By all human experience, Lazarus is past helping. Decay has begun to consume his body. Yet when Jesus calls his name, Lazarus experiences the restoration of strength, health, emotions, mobility, utility, purpose, and family. Jesus restores the infinite realm of Lazarus' possibility. In a similar way, Jesus can remove whatever barriers are between you and the restoration of your possibilities.

Jesus Can Deliver Us from Any Condition

You may say that although these testimonies of God's power are true, they seem separated from the resurrection of your personal possibility. Perhaps you feel that you were born with a disadvantage. Apparently denied things that others seem to enjoy, you feel void of certain emotional equipment. Your ability to navigate relationships and to deal with everyday stresses and challenges seems to have been lost at birth.

All conditions are either organic or spiritual in nature, which means that all conditions can be overcome through the power of God, who rules over both the natural and spiritual worlds. I want to encourage you that the duration of your condition, whether spiritual or physical, doesn't hinder God's ability to change it. Just because you have never felt joy, experienced peace, benefited from a balanced mind, or felt contentment doesn't mean that you never will. It is a matter of resurrection. Remember that Christ's relationship with you and the faith that you exercise in Him are founded on the principle of resurrection. Jesus is the *"resurrection, and the life"* (John 11:25). It is a matter of pressing through the barrier of human impossibility into the realm of faith and infinite possibility. The following story is an illustration of this truth.

> Just because you have never felt joy, peace, or contentment doesn't mean you never will.

"I Don't Want to Live Like This"

Often, we think that our attendance at an event is simply social until we realize that God desires to use us to assist someone whom we've never met before. I was attending a concert at a music workshop, and a choir of approximately eighty people was on the platform. Their white and gold robes were sparkling in the spotlights. The first few notes brought about ten thousand of the fifteen thousand people in attendance to their feet. The whole place was rocking with feet tapping and hands clapping. I was caught up in this when, suddenly, a young man asked me if the seat next to me was taken. When I told him that it wasn't, he sat down.

As the music came to an end, we exchanged positive comments about the choir's ministry. The choir moved into another song about God's ability to deliver us if we put our trust in Him. The woman singing the lead was anointed. The Spirit moved as the song's message touched people in the crowd. Tears, praises, shouts, and even a few agonizing screams were heard throughout the auditorium. The young man sitting next to me began to scream for God's help. He kept saying, "I don't want to live like this any longer."

The song ended, and the choir moved off the platform to make room for the next ministry. It must have been my suit that gave me away. The young man introduced himself to me as Darius and asked if I was a preacher. I admit that I battled with acknowledging that I was, because I just wanted to enjoy the concert. When I said yes, however, the music of the next choir became the background for an unexpected conversation.

Darius had been abused as a young child by one of his male relatives. As he grew older, he lived as a homosexual, first out of imitation and then out of a drive that he could not explain. His life, and the people that he was sexually involved with, became a blur. Darius accepted Christ, but continued to struggle with his lifestyle. He was even a musician at his church, but no one attempted to speak of his difficulty for fear of alienating him. He didn't think that his entrenched lifestyle would ever end. He saw people who were living other kinds of lives, but he had given up hope that his life would ever be any different. His behavior became even more risky out of desperation. He was both crying out for help and looking for a way to end it all. It was clear to him that he was lost.

"Does God Want Me This Way?"

Once again, I asked God for the right words. Then Darius asked the question, "Does God want me this way?" People had told him that he must have had homosexual tendencies from birth. He should simply accept his fate and adjust his expectations of family, fatherhood (in the traditional sense), and future. Yet something within him would occasionally begin to war against that advice.

I began by telling Darius that any behavior that is not in accordance with the will of God—including homosexuality—is a fruit of the flesh. The fire of his abusive experience had left him wounded with behavioral scars. That was why he was often depressed, defensive, fearful for his life, and suicidal. The more he had repeated the homosexual behavior, the more he had begun to identify himself by it, until his dreams of who he really wanted to be had almost vanished. His perception of his own character had been altered by his actions.

> Any behavior that is not in accordance with the will of God is a fruit of the flesh.

I explained to him that the abuse he had suffered was an attempt by his relative to pass on the agony of his own experience. This is one of the enemy's chief methods of perpetuating generational pain. I told Darius that Satan had achieved a victory up to that moment but that things were about to change. I saw that he had faith to be healed, and I spoke to the foundations, the beginnings, of his experience.

As we talked, however, we made a confusing discovery. Darius had mixed feelings about his past abuse and present lifestyle. On the one hand, he knew that it was destructive. On the other hand, through the years, he had learned, in some sense, to enjoy his experiences. Being involved in what is pleasurable but inappropriate is a chief characteristic of sin.

Most people have a difficult time admitting that something they enjoy is wrong. They rationalize their action in order to continue doing it. Darius felt that, besides his sinful behavior, something additional must be wrong with him because he did not totally hate his sin. I explained to him that many people enjoy and make excuses for their behavior until the holiness of God in them produces a righteous anger at it. The first step is obedience.

Power to Obey

The Holy Spirit gives us the power to obey God. Obedience can be effective in overcoming sin in our lives when we lack both faith and maturity. In behavioral issues, such as the one Darius faced, many people experience deliverance as a result of obedience before they reach full maturity in Christ. Just as children are sometimes too young to understand the value of their parents' rules and must obey "because Daddy said so," we have to trust that God's Word is true and good for our lives, and obey just because He has told us to.

One of the keys to obedience is to know and admit your weakness. You must understand that part of resisting temptation is staying away from a sinful activity rather than constantly exposing yourself to it. We often lose our judgment when we are in the midst of challenging emotional situations. Strong emotion can push our better judgment off a cliff. Jesus prayed that we would be kept from the evil of this world. (See John 17:15.) God will deliver us from our sinful behavior, but we must participate in our own deliverance by staying out of compromising situations until our faith, spiritual maturity, and habitual holiness enable us to resist sin. We have to develop immunity to sin because the world will continue to offer temptation that must be resisted.

Darius and I prayed for his healing and deliverance. Those sitting near us began to support our prayer with praise. I asked the Lord to step into the fire of his childhood experience and remove his sense of powerlessness. Then I rebuked the spirit of confusion that had plagued his life so that he could see himself the way God wanted him to. I prayed about the suicide that he had considered and his desire to end his life through his risky behavior. Though his early experience was not his fault, he could no longer use it as an excuse for his present lifestyle.

A Changed Destiny

The tone of Darius's voice changed. For some reason, I asked him his name, and he said that it was Daniel. Darius was the name that he'd adopted for himself. While it had distanced him from his past abuse, it had also locked him into his homosexuality. But his destiny was changing, and his voice reflected that reality. God was delivering him and giving him the life that he truly desired. I told him to let it go, that God had another life for him. Fear crept into his expression because the homosexual lifestyle was all that he had ever known. I told him that I saw within him the faith to be delivered. It was as if my words struck a chord in him.

The Word of God is greater than any situation, no matter how long the condition has existed. All Daniel needed was faith enough to be healed and delivered. I repeated the words of Jesus, *"According to your faith be it unto you"* (Matthew 9:29). I told him that I had faith for him. His life had been a den of lions bred to consume him, but he was still alive because God had preserved him in spite of all his attempts to destroy himself. He was about to be rescued by the Spirit and the Word of God.

Visualizing a New Life by Faith

I explained to Daniel that the devil's last weapon was the fear that he was feeling. The anointing that God had placed in his life included his healing and deliverance. Although the vessel of strength and hope was just about empty, he had to reach into that vessel by faith, and God would provide what he needed. I told him that his deliverance had been completed before God created the world. God knew him and saw his healing before he was born. *"I know the thoughts that I think toward you, saith the* Lord, *thoughts of peace, and not of evil, to give you an expected end"* (Jeremiah 29:11). Healing had always been available to him. He was not beyond hope and the power of God. God was waiting for him to discover the gift of his own freedom.

> Daniel thought that he'd been waiting for God, but God had been waiting for him.

Daniel thought that he'd been waiting for God, but God had been waiting for him. I asked him to visualize living the life that he desired: a life without fear, guilt, and the shame that he always felt. I told him to see his new life in his mind because, what the mind conceives, the will puts into action. I repeated the promises of health, strength, sufficiency, peace, and security that God gives us. I explained that the new man in Christ was the image that God had in store for him.

When we finished praying, I looked up and saw that all around us, people were weeping. They had listened and participated in Daniel's deliverance through their faith and prayers. The promises of God became the content of Daniel's new vision for himself. He began to scream, "I see it; I'm free." He started hugging everyone in sight, repeating, "I see it; I'm free. I see it; I'm free." His praise was contagious. People who didn't know exactly what had happened knew that something supernatural had occurred. Some watched in amazement, but the most amazed person was Daniel. God had resurrected his realm of possibility.

Your Pain Doesn't Fit You

You, also, can experience the resurrecting power of God for your emotional wounds and scars. His Word has the potency to overcome any condition. If you believe that things will never change, this may be keeping you from your deliverance. Perhaps, like Daniel, you have been waiting for God—but God has been waiting for you. He is ready to heal you without scars. He is waiting to see if you have the faith to be healed.

Tragic events in your life have threatened to destroy you. Some negative past involvement or event has loosed you from your strength, joy, self-esteem, and peace. People have attempted to rob you of your hope. Those close to you may have sown negative comments and discouragement in your heart, causing you to give up your dreams while leaving your faith wounded and your vision scarred. A feeling of sadness has attached itself to you so that it now seems to fit you like a well-worn coat.

> The house you were raised in does not have to define who you are.

Your pain may be comfortable and familiar to you, but it doesn't fit you because you are a child of God. Your heavenly Father wants to give you *"the garment of praise for the spirit of heaviness"* (Isaiah 61:3). Just as Moses did, you must discover that the house you were raised in does not have to define who you are. You have to take on your true identity. With the assistance of God, you can receive the transformation that you desire.

Faith Connects You with Resurrection Power

Because the Holy Spirit lives within us, you and I are walking around in active resurrection power. It is faith, however, that connects us to this power. The fundamental principle of deliverance is founded on God's ability to resurrect dead things. The length of inactivity and decomposition are of no concern to Him. If you have memorialized your wounds and scars with a gravestone, that won't hinder the power of God. It doesn't matter how long the stone has been in front of the grave. He is not restricted in any way by the declaration of death, just as He wasn't hindered when Lazarus was in the tomb for four days. Even if your problem has been in your family for generations, God's promises transcend generations and their associated conditions. The length of your condition will only testify to the greatness of His power. He who has promised is able to perform it. (See Romans 4:21.) He who has promised gives us the power to get up after everybody else has declared us dead.

Just Because It's Never Happened, Doesn't Mean It Never Will

I want to tell you the story of one other person whom the Scripture uses to encourage our faith when we have struggled under circumstances or a mind-set that seems to have lasted forever.

> *And there sat a certain man at Lystra, impotent in his feet, being a cripple from his mother's womb, who never had walked: The same heard Paul speak: who stedfastly beholding him, and perceiving that he had faith to be healed, said with a loud voice, Stand upright on thy feet. And he leaped and walked.* (Acts 14:8–10)

This man is sitting in a place that drains his strength and distorts his vision for himself and his perception of his personal opportunities. He has a desire to walk, he has seen others walk, but he himself has never walked. Some problem in his past that he had no control over prevents him from moving now. He wants to participate fully in life, but he can't. He has legs, but he lacks the strength to walk.

As an infant, perhaps he was able to turn over and crawl after a fashion, but as he grew older, his body could not do what he saw others doing. He didn't realize that something was missing in him until he tried to do what others seemed to do so easily. He remained in the same place of inability as he grew to adulthood, so that he has no other image of himself.

Like the lame man, something that happened early in your life may also be preventing you from fulfilling the desires of your heart—holding down a job, pursuing a dream, walking in integrity, or building significant relationships. Some of us know intrinsically that we were born incomplete, that something has been missing from our lives since birth. We are fully aware of our personal inabilities and disabilities, and we've learned how to live with them. Not liking how we feel, we've adjusted our expectations by surrounding ourselves with others who have similar problems or with those who will not challenge our issues. We've simply accepted the fact that we will never feel any differently. Sometimes, in order to survive, we whisper to ourselves that nothing is wrong, when we are actually totally dissatisfied with ourselves.

When we have made the decision to live with our inability, we begin to call it something that sounds "acceptable" to both others and ourselves. We may actively seek the approval of others as a form of validation. As we continue to validate the negative, however, we slowly come to the revelation that something within us has died.

Often, if we're not excusing our actions, we're blaming others for them. Yet shifting blame suspends us in the same emotional place. The initial hurt may not have been our fault, but we can control what we do about it in the future. Often, it's easier to blame the consequences on someone else than to take positive action for ourselves.

After the first humans disobeyed God in the garden of Eden, they perfected the art of shifting the cause of the consequences away from themselves. Eve blamed the serpent, while Adam blamed Eve and even God Himself. But shifting the blame didn't remove the effects of their actions. They were separated from the place that God had provided for them, which removed them from the perfect will of God for their lives. (See Genesis 3:11–13; 17–19.)

> **Shifting the blame can't remove the effects of our actions.**

Losing contact with our provision often occurs so quietly that we don't notice that it has happened until a situation arises that requires an ability that died inside us a long time ago. We watch others change, progress emotionally, and enter the next dimension of promise, while we stay the same. Let me assure you of something based on the resurrection power of God: Just because you've never done it before doesn't mean that you never will. What you went through or what you're struggling with has no effect on the power of God because His power supersedes the presence of any hindrance in your life. When you are saved and filled with the Holy Spirit, no hindrance can stay in the presence of your anointing.

Hearing the Word

The lame man, who has never walked in his entire life, is able to walk after exercising faith in the power of God. How did this occur? First, *"this man heard Paul speaking"* (Acts 14:9 NKJV). Paul is preaching the power of God in Lystra. He speaks a word of faith that stirs something within the man that he has never felt before. He hears a word that supernaturally attacks his disability, a word that is greater than his condition. This gets his full attention. The transforming power of God begins to fight what the man has felt his entire life. The word you receive is a critical element in the fulfillment of your purpose. This is why it is important who teaches or preaches to you. You need to fill your heart and mind with the Word of God, which will attack the foundations of the negative issues in your life.

Having Faith for Healing

Second, the Bible says that Paul observes the man intently and sees that he has the faith to be healed (v. 9). The Scripture doesn't gloss over the man's condition. The text says that he was *"impotent in his feet, being a cripple from his mother's womb, who never had walked"* (v. 8). This verse reminds me of the fact that, although we were birthed into salvation, we still have some form of "lameness" because we need to be delivered from our emotional wounds and scars. If emotional lameness could have prevented our new birth, many of us would never have been born. We are truly born again, but we aren't experiencing the full power of Christ. We are waiting for a word that will address our conditions.

Like the lame man, faith will connect us to our deliverance. When the man hears of the power of God, he knows that his opportunity has arrived. Forgetting his condition, he begins to stir in his position. Paul, knowing that signs and wonders follow the Word, *"said with a loud voice, Stand up straight on your feet! And he leaped and walked"* (v. 10).

Paul speaks in a loud voice; it is a command. Now that the faith connection has been made, Paul is speaking directives, not requests. It seems as if Paul is speaking to the man's feet, but he is actually speaking to the man's faith. Sometimes, you have to speak encouraging words to your own faith. The apostle commands the man's faith to do what his legs and feet have never done. If the man could have spoken to himself and caused this change, he would have done so long before this, but his feet couldn't go where his faith wouldn't take him. It's faith that moves mountains, and *"faith cometh by hearing, and hearing by the word of God"* (Romans 10:17).

> We don't do anything that we don't first visualize in our minds.

The years of lameness drained the man's strength and dissolved his ability to see himself changed. His mind was darkened. He saw himself only as a lame man sitting in the same place, but God saw him differently. When the power of God connects with the man's faith, light begins invading the dark place of his mind called Never Done It Before. God's Word brings light to the dark places in our understanding. The place within the man that has never lived or that has gone dark begins to experience light. He starts to see himself in a way that he has never before envisioned himself.

Again, we don't do anything that we don't first visualize in our minds. For most things, this visualization is so habitual and happens so quickly that we often don't even notice it.

The place of visualization was dark in the lame man's mind. He saw others walking, and he thought about walking, but he couldn't see himself moving. Paul begins speaking to his faith, knowing that faith will bring light to his vision of himself and that he will begin to see himself walking.

How can he see himself walking if he's never walked before? People pass by him each day. He knows what it looks like to walk. Imitation is the precursor of any accomplishment. By watching others, he knows that there is something that God has equipped him to do that lies dormant within him.

Paul's vision of the man's healing forces light into the lame man's vision of himself. Through the eyes of faith, the apostle sees him healed before he receives his healing. Paul probably smiled in anticipation because he saw him without his lameness, breaking through the barrier of his disability while receiving strength to be loosed from the place of his confinement.

Light in Your Dark Places

As Paul did for the lame man, I am speaking to your faith, not your condition. I am speaking as loudly as possible into your spirit. Your season of weakness, impotence, anxiety, financial distress, depression, joblessness, homelessness, anger, or whatever it is that you are facing can't stand against faith in God. I declare strength to your faith and light to the dark places in your life experience. By faith, God is creating light in the places that trial, testing, and disappointment have made dark.

Again, I am not speaking to your dysfunction; I'm speaking to your faith. God's rule is, *"According to your faith be it unto you"* (Matthew 9:29), not "According to your condition be it unto you." The devil would like you to believe that your condition dictates your future. God says your future is not according to your struggle; it's according to your faith.

Jesus taught His disciples how to move mountains. He said, *"Have faith in God"* (Mark 11:22). Jesus was teaching us that, no matter what the situation, we are to believe God. In spite of your past experiences and present challenges, therefore, *believe God.*

I want you to see yourself as I see you: blessed, delivered, prosperous, and healed without scars. The infinite realm of possibility became God's reality for the lame man. God wants to do the same thing for you. Will you stand up? The components of your deliverance from the scars of life are in place: The Word of God, your faith, and the power of the Holy Spirit have positioned you to respond to the voice of God. God has spoken something that you've never heard before, shown you something that you've never seen before, and revealed something that you've never conceived before so that He can do something in your life that He's never done before. It's time to stand upright on your feet.

> I want you to see yourself as I see you: blessed, delivered, and healed without scars.

When you respond by faith, an entirely new realm of possibility opens up to you. Despite the troubles of your past, God desires to restore your hope, joy, strength, and faith in Him. He is a faithful and loving Father who wants to reestablish your potential while revealing His brand new possibilities for your life. Remember—just because you've never done it before, doesn't mean you never will. Now is the time of your deliverance. Stand up!

Chapter Eleven

Reach Out to Jesus

————————◆————————

*Our wounds and scars position us to make contact
with God's healing power.*

When I was a boy, my friends and I would go to the pool in the summer and play our usual games, such as trying to hold each other under the water for as long as possible. We took special pleasure in jumping into the pool just in time to keep our friends from struggling to the surface for air. Looking back on it, it was an absolutely crazy way for us to enjoy ourselves. I have often wondered why things that appear so foolish now that I am older seemed like so much fun when I was a kid.

Of course, we played all our games in the deep end of the pool. It gave us an exciting sense of danger, and we never gave much thought to the fact that there was more than enough water for fun to become fatal. Sometimes, one of us would stay underwater for an extra long time to give the others the impression that we were in real distress.

Chip could hold his breath longer than anyone I knew. He and I were both lifeguards at a summer camp and felt very confident in the water. Chip was one of those kids whose physique was sculpted at a very early age. He was extremely muscular and was clearly the strongest of us. He excelled at every sport he attempted. We felt that he had an unfair genetic advantage over us or that his mother had found a unique way to feed him that produced muscles. We all wanted to eat at his house. He said it was from drinking milk, but we didn't believe him. Later, we found out that he'd suffered a childhood disease and that the doctors had prescribed steroids during his recovery. He had gone into the hospital looking like a relatively normal kid, but he had come out looking like Hercules.

Reaching Out for Deliverance

I remember that the pool was extremely crowded one day when Chip dove to the bottom and actually stood and waved at us as we looked at his distorted image at the bottom of the pool. For some reason, we had all decided to gather at the edge of the water to see how long he could hold out this time. At first, it looked as if he was attempting to sit on the bottom of the pool, further demonstrating his breath-holding dominance over the rest of us. The other boys began to laugh, but something didn't seem quite right to me. Then I saw Chip struggle and attempt to come to the surface. The laughter gradually silenced as, one by one, the boys realized that something was wrong.

I dove in. When I reached Chip, his face held an expression that I still cannot fully describe. It was a mixture of terror, disbelief, and exertion. He was struggling with all his might to free his foot, which was caught in the grating. Being in the water slowed all our movements and muted our communication. I reached for him, but he didn't seem to see me as he continued to concentrate on his toes in the grate.

I attempted to grab Chip around the waist. He was pulling violently now, as if he had made a decision to sacrifice his toes, if need be. He was past his limit, and I was quickly reaching mine. I pulled on his shoulders and arms while he concentrated on tugging at his foot, so that we were actually pulling against one another. In desperation, he finally abandoned his own efforts and reached out for me. I gripped his hands and did for him what he couldn't do for himself. As I pulled, his foot came free. We made it out alive that day because, as I reached for him, he reached for me. His effort helped me to release him from the thing that was positioning him for a loss of life, purpose, promise, and destiny.

> We try to deliver ourselves by our own methods instead of reaching out for Jesus.

Drawing Close to Jesus during Stormy Times

Chip's ordeal is a picture of what happens to us when we try to deliver ourselves from our wounds and scars by our own methods instead of reaching out for Jesus. The Savior demonstrated this truth to His disciples one stormy night.

Jesus made His disciples get into the boat and go before Him to the other side, while He sent the multitudes away. And when He had sent the multitudes away, He went up on the mountain by Himself to pray. Now when evening came, He was alone there. But the boat was now in the middle of the sea, tossed by the waves, for the wind was contrary. Now in the fourth watch of the night Jesus went to them, walking on the sea. And when the disciples saw Him walking on the sea, they were troubled, saying, "It is a ghost!" And they cried out for fear. But immediately Jesus spoke to them, saying, "Be of good cheer! It is I; do not be afraid." And Peter answered Him and said, "Lord, if it is You, command me to come to You on the water." So He said, "Come." And when Peter had come down out of the boat, he walked on the water to go to Jesus. But when he saw that the wind was boisterous, he was afraid; and beginning to sink he cried out, saying, "Lord, save me!" And immediately Jesus stretched out His hand and caught him, and said to him, "O you of little faith, why did you doubt?" And when they got into the boat, the wind ceased. Then those who were in the boat came and worshiped Him, saying, "Truly You are the Son of God." (Matthew 14:22–33 NKJV)

When we read this passage, we usually focus on Christ walking on the water, and Peter, the lone disciple who has enough faith, being encouraged to step out of the boat and walk with Him. I think, however, that there is a greater message for us here. I don't think that the command to come was exclusive to Peter, but that Jesus was addressing the entire boatload of disciples. I believe that the Lord's profound desire was that they learn to draw closer to Him in the stormy circumstances of life.

> The Lord desires that we draw closer to Him in the stormy circumstances of life.

Life's Storms Challenge Our Ability to Cope

The disciples were experienced fishermen and knew how to handle a boat. This means that they were struggling to control something with which they already had expertise.

Emotional turmoil can cause us to wrestle with everyday activities that should be second nature to us. What used to be doable becomes difficult. For example, we may find it hard to go to work, keep house, or raise our children.

The storms connected to the wounds and scars we've received in the past can disrupt and delay the fulfillment of our God-given destinies for years. As we look into the seeming darkness of the future, we hope that someone will come along and rescue us by providing the answers we seek. We seem positioned halfway between the will of God and the past that we are trying to leave behind, finding ourselves caught between two powerful forces. On one side, the will of God is pushing us toward our destinies, while on the other, our stormy emotions call us back to the origins of our discontent and disappointment.

> When we are pressed to the end of our strength, we are at the threshold of our deliverance.

The wind blowing against the disciples was *"contrary"* (Matthew 14:24), and as the intensity of the storm increased, their struggle increased. I think that each disciple faced a personal storm as he strained to keep the boat under control. Out alone in the dark tempest, the disciples probably felt isolated from the rest of the world and even from one another as they dealt with their internal fears.

The Bible describes them as *"toiling"* (Mark 6:48). The Greek word for *"toiling"* is *basanizo*, which means "to torture: pain, toil, torment, toss, vex." (See *Strong's* #G928.) The strength of the disciples' resolve, will, and faith was being fully tested. They were at their breaking point. However, they didn't realize that when they were pressed to the end of their strength, they were at the threshold of their deliverance. The same is true for us.

Failing to Recognize Jesus and His Power to Save

When Jesus came walking on the water in the midst of the storm, the disciples were troubled instead of inspired at the sight of Him. They were terrified, thinking that He was a ghost, and they cried out in fear.

The disciples didn't recognize Jesus in the storm. Likewise, our past disappointments, traumas, and tragedies can diminish our ability to recognize that Jesus is in fact with us during our troubles and that He has the power to deliver us. As we face each new problem, we act as if He can't handle the situation or as if He must prove Himself to us anew, instead of trusting in His love and protection. On one occasion, Jesus sadly asked one of His disciples, *"Have I been so long time with you, and yet hast thou not known me, Philip?"* (John 14:9).

The disciples failed to recognize Jesus in the storm because their perception of their own negative condition had clouded their perception of Him as healer and deliverer. It had also caused them to forget that Jesus had already provided the resources for their deliverance. He had given His followers the power to meet various challenges as well as to heal and deliver people: *"Behold, I give unto you power to tread on serpents and scorpions, and over all the power of the enemy: and nothing shall by any means hurt you"* (Luke 10:19). That same power was available to them, but they forgot who Jesus really was and experienced a loss of ability to help themselves through His power.

Mark 6:52 says that they hadn't expected Jesus to save them because *"they considered not the miracle of the loaves: for their heart was hardened."* Just before they had gotten into the boat, Jesus had performed the miracle of the loaves and fish, feeding five thousand people. (See Mark 6:36–44.) Yet this incident had already faded in their memory. The revelation of Jesus' ability to address the needs of every man, woman, boy, and girl had escaped them. They had accepted the miracle, but didn't consider its full implications. Perhaps they believed that this miracle was the extent of Jesus' power and authority.

> Jesus has the ability to address the needs of every man, woman, boy, and girl.

Because their hearts were hardened, they were limited in their faith and didn't trust Him for their present needs.

Will Jesus Pass Us By?

Mark 6:48 says that Jesus *"would have passed by them,"* but He responded when His disciples cried out. Was He unconcerned about their dilemma? No, the disciples were never out of the Lord's watchful care. The same verse says that the Lord *"saw them toiling in rowing"* (Mark 6:48). Perhaps He wanted to see if they would use the faith and power that God had given them not only to weather the storm, but also to overcome it.

At times, it may seem as if Jesus is in no hurry to reach us when we are in emotional turmoil. He may almost seem casual in His approach, as if our difficulties are not of much concern to Him. One of the great hindrances to emotional deliverance is a tendency to forget the words of promise that Jesus has spoken. He has made a commitment to us. He will not only meet us on the other side of our adversity, but He will also walk through it with us.

Have you asked yourself if Jesus cares about your needs? The Bible says that He is *"a man of sorrows, and acquainted with* grief" (Isaiah 53:3). Be assured that He cares, and that He is paying close attention to your struggle. When the reality of our problems distorts our perception of the reality of His ability to deliver us, however, fear moves in, and our faith wavers.

As We Step Out in Faith, the Storm May Worsen

The disciples were afraid of losing their lives in the storm. Jesus understood that fear had overcome their faith, and He immediately addressed the heart of the problem. He encouraged them by saying, *"Be of good cheer; it is I; be not afraid"* (Matthew 14:27). His words calmed their fears while resurrecting their trust in Him. Note that the Lord had not yet taken His disciples out of the tempest. He addressed their fears while they were still in the storm.

Sometimes, a kind of recklessness born of love and faith is needed for deliverance. When Peter requested to join Jesus on the sea, he was saying, in effect, "Now that You've addressed my fear, tell me to come closer to You." Peter may have been the disciple with the greatest desire for deliverance from his fear. In order to be delivered, however, he had to get closer to Jesus. Yet, while he was challenging his own fear, stepping out in faith, and acting on the Word of God, he began sinking! Things appear to have worsened when he drew closer to the Lord.

This is a vital reminder for us that, as we seek to reach out to Jesus to overcome our wounds and scars, the storm of emotional conflict is likely to increase. One of the difficulties that we will face is our own emotional opposition to our healing. Our emotional wounds will seem to have more power than the Word of God, even after the process of our deliverance has begun. We will step out in faith, believing the Word of God, but then conflicting emotions, which war against our faith, will rise up in opposition.

This storm will attempt to toss us between deliverance and denial, correction and conflict, faith and fear. The winds of our emotions and the waves of uncertainty will appear to become more intense. Yet, when fear and depression pull us farther into the wounded place in our emotions, we must cry out for Jesus and allow Him to reach out and rescue us.

Cry Out for Jesus in Faith

As Peter sinks, he calls out for Jesus. He has enough faith to know that the Savior will respond to his cry. When your cry contains the essence of your pain, be assured that He hears. Rather than trying to fix things yourself or rely on past experiences, call on Jesus. Desperation works for our good when it causes us to express the voice of resurrected faith.

> We should always hold on to Jesus in the storms of life, and never let go.

Jesus reaches out, catches Peter, and walks him back to the boat in the storm. It's important to remember that, at this point, the winds hadn't ceased and the waves continued to roll. We should always hold on to Jesus in the storms of life, and never let go. He will never leave or forsake us. (See Hebrews 13:5.)

Jesus Will Calm Our Storms

In the midst of the disciples' toiling, Jesus walks over to the boat and gets in, and the wind suddenly ceases. The Bible says that *"they were sore amazed in themselves beyond measure, and wondered"* (Mark 6:51). Our wounds can become so severe and our scars so vivid that we begin to believe that no relief is possible. We lose faith that God has the power to help us in such a personal way. The wounds have birthed such intense negative feelings that they feel too powerful to overcome.

The extent of the disciple's amazement and wonder indicates how little faith they had to be delivered. Again, their emotions didn't allow them to consider the other miracles of Jesus that they had witnessed. It is common for intense emotion to blind us to past instances of the faithfulness and power of God. The present trial that the disciples faced blocked their perception of Christ's sovereignty over all things.

Note that the disciples gladly received Him into the boat. This is the same Jesus who was unrecognizable to them just minutes before. Yet His presence and words cause their faith to stir and courage to rise within them. They begin to remember who He is and what He has done for them and others in the past. In the midst of our trials, we need to seek His presence and encourage ourselves by remembering His faithfulness.

Participating in God's Healing Process

As we reach out to Jesus, we have to participate in the healing of our wounds and scars. The following account from the life of David teaches us how to cooperate with Him during this process. David went through a time when he was caught up in an emotional storm. He had committed adultery with Bathsheba and exploited his kingly authority by having her husband, Uriah, slain. Now he and Bathsheba have had a child out of wedlock.

Repent of Any Sin

David is depressed and disappointed in himself. He attempts to cover his sin until Nathan the prophet convicts him through the story of a man who owns only one little sheep, which is a pet to his children. His lamb is taken and killed by a rich and powerful man, just because the rich man doesn't want to use his own sheep for a feast he is holding. David is incensed at the injustice, yet Nathan tells him that the story is really about him. He is guilty of robbing what belongs to another man and killing him. David immediately repents of his sin.

David and Bathsheba's baby, however, becomes very sick. This is God's judgment for David's disobedience, adultery, and murder. David fasts and prays for days, hoping that God will heal the child. He wants God to bless the mess he has made.

Accept God's Forgiveness, and Offer Him Praise

Then David's servants tell him that the child has died, and he reacts in a remarkable way. He fully accepts the Lord's discipline and picks himself up from his depression. The Bible tells us that he *"arose...and washed"* (2 Samuel 12:20). This action could be considered a symbol of forgiveness offered and received. David wrote about his experience in Psalm 32:3–5:

> *When I kept silence, my bones waxed old through my roaring all the day long. For day and night thy hand was heavy upon me: my moisture is turned into the drought of summer. I acknowledged my sin unto thee, and mine iniquity have I not hid. I said, I will confess my transgressions unto the* Lord; *and thou forgavest the iniquity of my sin.*

David has begun to exchange the ashes of his disobedience and emotional trial for the beauty of a renewed relationship with God. He then *"anointed himself"* (2 Samuel 12:20). I believe that this anointing is a symbol of gladness and restoration. He exchanges his depression for the oil of joy. He also changes his clothes. David's mourning clothes represented his emotional state. Another exchange is being made. He puts on a new garment, as if replacing his heavy heart for one filled with praise. Then he goes into the house of worship. He enters the Lord's *"gates with thanksgiving, and...his courts with praise"* (Psalm 100:4). (See 2 Samuel 11–12.)

David discovered one of the key ingredients of deliverance from emotional wounds and scars: Deliverance is possible only if you participate in the process. You must decide to actively exchange your mourning, depression, anxiety, and ashes for the praise, beauty, forgiveness, and joy of the Lord by reaching out for His promise of restoration.

> Deliverance is possible only if you participate in the process.

Develop "Positive Frustration"

The "garments" of your depression, fear, and anxiety are old and ragged; they are ready for the trash heap. You must commit yourself to removing the garments that represent the scars and wounds of your life. Each time these garments present themselves, you must replace them with the things of God. The Bible says, *"Whatsoever things are true, whatsoever things are honest, whatsoever things are just, whatsoever things are pure, whatsoever things are lovely, whatsoever things are of good report; if there be any virtue, and if there be any praise, think on these things"* (Philippians 4:8).

As you grow weary of your negative thoughts and feelings, a "positive" frustration will begin grow within you. This frustration is the genesis for change in your life. Positive frustration births new beginnings. Haven't there been times in your life when frustration became the seed of change? You were fed up with something in your life, and you began to sincerely look for a better way to live, a better place to work, or a more edifying place to worship. When you reach the point of being "sick and tired" of something, a new determination is usually born. Sometimes, we feel we can't stand it if change is delayed another day.

Perceive Your Anointing

David was able to pick himself up, forgive himself, declare personal joy, and worship the Lord wholeheartedly because he understood that God's hand was upon his life. He knew that he was God's chosen vessel. The Bible says there was a point after Samuel anointed him that David's perception of his anointing crystallized. *"David **perceived** that the Lord had established him king over Israel, and that he had exalted his kingdom for his people Israel's sake"* (2 Samuel 5:12, emphasis added).

> **Have you perceived who you are in Christ?**

Have you perceived who you are in Christ? The Scripture calls you *"a chosen generation, a royal priesthood, an holy nation, a peculiar people; that ye should show forth the praises of him who hath called you out of darkness into his marvellous light"* (1 Peter 2:9). A personal revelation of the power of God operating in your life will give you the strength to move past the reality of your wounded past and help you to overcome your scar-induced behavior.

Real issues need real solutions. The help that many people offer is theoretical or hypothetical so that the outcome is never guaranteed. Yet the Bible says that God is able to perform everything that He has promised. (See Romans 4:21.) He has made power available to you that is equal to whatever circumstances you face. You must touch the power of God by reaching for Jesus. If you reach for Him, then you will make contact with grace, mercy, and power. The Father's touch will heal your wounds and remove your scars.

Going through life with the burden of past failures can be extremely defeating. You must decide right now that your wounds have been open long enough. The time has come for you to push through defeat, disappointment, rejection, tradition, and opinion until you have touched God. Perhaps you have tried to do this through other supposed methods of deliverance, but were disappointed. Thoughts of "Why try again?" repeatedly creep into your mind. *Try again.* When you reach out to God, it will be worth all the effort of the past.

The Woman Who Pushed Past Her Issue

The Bible tells of a woman who has to push past many things in order to touch Jesus and receive her healing and deliverance.

> *A certain woman, which had an issue of blood twelve years, and had suffered many things of many physicians, and had spent all that she had, and was nothing bettered, but rather grew worse, when she had heard of Jesus, came in the press behind, and touched his garment. For she said, If I may touch but his clothes, I shall be whole.* (Mark 5:25–28)

This woman has suffered from a debilitating bleeding condition for much of her life. Her condition has restricted her from social interaction, leaving her with a feeling of limited possibilities. It is affecting everything about her—the way she thinks, feels, and sees herself. It rules her life. She has done all that she can within her own power to effect a change, but nothing has worked.

The woman's desperation and hopelessness have apparently increased to the point that she no longer cares what people think about her, or how many times she has already tried and failed to fix her own problem. She hears that Help has arrived in her city, and she decides to press her way to Him. She pushes past the thought that she is wasting her time because there is something different in her anticipation that day. She feels that destiny hinges on her ability to reach out to Jesus, so she begins to repeat to herself her need to simply touch Him.

Perhaps she has realized that there is no use in berating herself for failing to find an answer to her condition before this. Self-victimization will not bring her closer to a solution. Placing blame on others also will do nothing to heal her condition. The problem must still be addressed, whether the fault is hers or someone else's. At this point in her life, the knowledge of what caused her affliction or what has perpetuated it is of little value. All she wants is wholeness.

As she makes her way to Jesus, perhaps the pain of the past and the disappointments of the present try to drown out her determination. I imagine that she keeps telling herself to push until she can reach for Him. As usual, there are obstacles to contend with. Not only is there the barrier of her chronic condition, but there is also the barrier of a massive crowd that surrounds Jesus.

Carried along to Jesus

Maybe the woman didn't anticipate the crowd, but God did. If you have been in the midst of a large crowd that is pressing in one direction and have been carried along by it, you can appreciate what I imagine happened next. Because the woman is physically weak, the crowd presents an impassable barrier to her. She has to reach Jesus, however, so she *"came in the press behind* [Him]" (Mark 5:27). Traditionally, interpreters depict her crawling to touch the hem of Jesus' garment, but I picture it differently. The word *"press"* in the Greek is the word *ochlos,* which means "a throng (as borne along)," and which is derived from a root word meaning "vehicle." (See *Strong's,* #G3793.)

This definition conveys a powerful image to me. I think the woman was jostled and propelled forward in the press. Too weak to resist the flow and force of the crowd, she is taken closer and closer to Jesus. Can you imagine how her excitement must have increased as the crowd that she first thought would keep her from Jesus actually carried her closer to Him?

> Our emotional wounds and scars push us toward Jesus.

We can apply this idea to our own circumstances. The emotional wounds and scars from the rejection, abuse, and disappointment that we have experienced seem to block our ability to receive healing and deliverance. Yet these are the very things that will push us toward Jesus. Our pain becomes the vehicle that positions us to make contact with the healing power of God! The woman accepted her dilemma and knew that Jesus was the only one who had an answer for her. Similarly, if you have accepted the reality of both the disappointments of the past and the power of Jesus, then you have entered the vehicle that God will use to transport you to your healing.

I believe that, as the crowd moves the woman closer to Jesus, her faith and strength increase in anticipation. She see glimpses of Him as the ebb and flow of the crowd continually shifts. Then, as she reaches the edge of the crowd, she gathers herself for the opportunity that she has waited for during twelve long years. The hem of His robe is her target. Fighting fatigue, she prepares to exchange the rags of her condition for the garment of her deliverance.

The woman understands that she is in the presence of God, and she kneels down and touches the hem of His garment. There are many other robes in the crowd, but it is His that she must touch. For her, time stands still as she reaches from where she is to where He is. She reaches from her past to her future. She reaches beyond her condition and into her healing, connecting the disappointment of the past with His power to transform her future. She reaches for *Him*, and His power responds to her.

*And straightway the fountain of her blood was dried up; and she felt in her body that she was healed of that plague. And Jesus, immediately knowing in himself that virtue had gone out of him, turned him about in the press, and said, Who touched my clothes? And his disciples said unto him, Thou seest the multitude thronging thee, and sayest thou, Who touched me? And he looked round about to see her that had done this thing. But the woman fearing and trembling, knowing what was done in her, came and fell down before him, and told him all the truth. And he said unto her, Daughter, **thy faith hath made thee whole**; go in peace, and be whole of thy plague.* (Mark 5:29–34, emphasis added)

The Bible says that, immediately after she touches Jesus, her condition dries up. She feels in her body that she is healed of the issue that has plagued her for twelve years. She has experienced virtue released by grace. Jesus then asks a rather unusual question. In a crowd of people straining to get near Him, He asks, "Who touched Me?" Her touch was different from all of the others in the crowd because God's power responds to faith.

Coming for the Right Reasons

People come to Jesus for a variety of reasons. Some desire to say that they have seen or touched Him. They are satisfied merely with touching Jesus, so they receive no touch from Him. Imagine the situation. There were dozens, perhaps hundreds, of people in close proximity to deliverance, yet they didn't receive a miracle. After the woman explained to Jesus what she had done, many people probably walked away realizing that they had missed an opportunity. They had been in the crowd for the wrong reasons. I'm sure that each person in that crowd had a need. Yet Jesus does not respond just to needs. He responds to faith.

> Jesus does not respond just to needs. He responds to faith.

Jesus has deep compassion for our problems, but He knows that faith is the road to wholeness in our lives. That is why He doesn't respond to mountains, blindness, storms, paralysis, or any other condition. Remember that He didn't say, "According to your need be it unto you," but rather, *"According to your faith be it unto you"* (Matthew 9:29). The woman with the issue reached for Jesus by faith, and grace responded to her. Faith gets the Lord's attention. As He tells the woman that she is well, He says, *"Be whole"* (Mark 5:34). She received complete healing and deliverance because she reached for Him out of a heart full of trust, and He reached back to her in response to her faith.

Reach Out to Jesus

The woman with the issue of blood was determined to get close to Jesus so that she could touch Him. She made an effort based on faith, ignored the obstacles, and pressed on until she was able to receive a blessing from God. If you have endured frustration, denial, fear, and disappointment, but are willing to press through these things to reach Jesus, then you are in the perfect position for a breakthrough.

God has made a choice for you. His choice is that you be blessed, healed, and delivered from the wounds and scars of your experiences. Now He is waiting for you to choose Him. His promises are a declaration of the expectations, rights, privileges, and opportunities that He has granted you. The Father looks at your difficulty from a position of power because He can do something about your scars. When you are hopeless about your situation, it is because you are looking at it from a position of fear and weakness.

> God has made a choice for you. Now He is waiting for you to choose Him.

When you reach out, and the intensity of your struggle increases, you must realize how close you are to deliverance. Isolation in harsh conditions can drain the strength out of your hope and faith. At these times, it is easy to bottom out emotionally. But at the bottom of every emotional valley is a brook. God has promised to be with you in the valley. (See Psalm 23:4.) He is committed to providing you with whatever you need, no matter what conditions or situations you are facing. You've waited long enough. Press into His presence where fullness waits. If you reach for Jesus, He will reach for you.

The Lord told Paul, *"My grace is sufficient for thee: for my strength is made perfect in weakness"* (2 Corinthians 12:9). Your own ability has its limits, but God's ability knows no limit. As dim as the future may seem to you, He sees your future in a completely different way. Allow your wounds and scars to press you toward the Great Physician so you may receive healing and restoration.

Chapter Twelve

Get Ready for the Harvest

Your wounds and scars are not a signal of defeat,
but an invitation to victory.

The Bible says that there are times and seasons for the fulfillment of the work of God. The manifestation of a specific promise, such as God's pledge to Abraham concerning the birth of Isaac, awaits a time or circumstance when no one but God can claim to have fulfilled it. Abraham and Sarah were well past childbearing age and Sarah had been barren for her entire life before their miracle child was born. Who but God could enable a 100-year-old man and a 90-year-old woman to have a child naturally? We have to trust God for the fulfillment of these promises in His time.

The healing of our wounds and scars also comes in due season. Perhaps you are discouraged because your heart's desire has not yet come about. Remember that just because you haven't done something or haven't been freed from something, doesn't mean you never will. *"For the vision is yet for **an appointed time**, but at the end it shall speak, and not lie: though* *it tarry, wait for it; because **it will surely come**, it will not tarry"* (Habakkuk 2:3, emphasis added).

God is working on your heart as well as your circumstances to bring you deliverance. Because He works through the principles that He has set forth in His Word, I know that some of you are overdue for your deliverance. You just don't realize it! You've been waiting too long because you haven't yet grasped the biblical concept of seasons of growth and seasons of harvest. I want to show you how you can release your harvest. We have to perceive and cooperate with the ways of God so we can begin to walk in the seasons that have already been ordained for our lives.

A Divinely Ordered Plan

In the physical world, God has established a rhythm that characterizes our seasons. *"While the earth remaineth, seedtime and harvest, and cold and heat, and summer and winter, and day and night shall not cease"* (Genesis 8:22). I believe that spiritual seasons also come in cycles. The Bible says, *"To every thing there is a season, and a time to every purpose under the heaven"* (Ecclesiastes 3:1).

> Spiritual seasons are both appointed times and appropriate times.

A spiritual season is the unfolding of a plan divinely ordered by God from the beginning of the world. It covers a period of time overseen by God and worked out in the lives of His people. The Scripture says, *"Known unto God are all his works from the beginning of the world"* (Acts 15:18). Spiritual seasons are both appointed times and appropriate times—appointed because they are set by God, and appropriate because they are suitable for the person's life, situation, and level of spiritual growth. Paul wrote, *"At his **appointed season** [God] brought his word [regarding eternal life through Christ] to light through the preaching entrusted to me by the command of God our Savior"* (Titus 1:3 NIV, emphasis added).

The Role of Growth and Fruit-Bearing

There are times of dormancy, growth, and fruit bearing in our lives. Psalm 1:1–3 says,

> *Blessed is the man that walketh not in the counsel of the ungodly, nor standeth in the way of sinners, nor sitteth in the seat of the scornful. But his delight is in the law of the LORD; and in his law doth he meditate day and night. And he shall be like a tree planted by the rivers of water, that **bringeth forth his fruit in his season; his leaf also shall not wither; and whatsoever he doeth shall prosper.*** (emphasis added)

God brings us to spiritual maturity and productivity. He sees us as trees planted by the river or, to put it another way, by *"rivers of living water"* (John 7:38). Jesus said, *"He that believeth on me, as the scripture hath said, out of his belly shall flow rivers of living water"* (v. 38). These rivers refer to the Holy Spirit. The Spirit nourishes us as we are planted firmly in God's Word, so that our lives naturally yield spiritual fruit and prosperity. We need to understand and fulfill the seasons God has ordained for us.

Hosea 6:3 says, *"Then shall we know, if we follow on to know the LORD: his going forth is prepared as the morning ["is as certain as the dawn" NASB]; and he shall come unto us as the rain, as the latter and former rain unto the earth."* This Scripture tells us that God's coming to us is as predictable as the rising of the sun. He will come to us as rain, relieving our parched lives and making us grow and bear fruit. When we look for our deliverance, we shouldn't be looking for it in terms of money, a house, a certain job, and so on. We should be looking for it in God Himself because, if He rains on us, then everything that He promised will also come to us.

What is the rain of God? Again, it is His Holy Spirit. If you are a believer in Jesus Christ, then the Spirit dwells within you, and you are being rained on. You are in a position to enter a new season, especially if you prepare the ground of your heart by yielding to God and obeying His Word. Your leaf will not wither and you will produce fruit at the right time.

> If you are a believer in Jesus Christ, you are being rained on.

Yes, we still have the dry seasons and the stormy seasons of life, but we also know that the seasons change and that harvesttime will come. These other seasons prepare us for what God wants to do in our lives. It is impossible to go through a summer without a winter. Rainy seasons bring us life-giving nourishment and refreshment, while harvest seasons bring us the results of the Spirit's workings in our inner lives.

The book of Isaiah also talks about God's ways in terms of rain. It says that God's Word will prosper where He sends it, just as rain initiates a course of physical provision for us: It waters the seed that is lying dormant in the earth and causes wheat to spring up, which is made into bread to sustain us:

As the rain cometh down, and the snow from heaven, and returneth not thither, but watereth the earth, and maketh it bring forth and bud, that it may give seed to the sower, and bread to the eater: so shall my word be that goeth forth out of my mouth: it shall not return unto me void, but it shall accomplish that which I please, and it shall prosper in the thing whereto I sent it. (Isaiah 55:10–11)

Harmony and Disharmony

There is harmony in the cycle of the seasons of our lives: We grow, mature, and bear fruit regularly as we are planted in the Word of God, are watered by His Spirit, and bear the fruit of His character. Yet this harmony can be disrupted. Adam and Eve were made in the image of God and given dominion, authority, and power to tend the garden of Eden and rule the earth. At the beginning, they dwelt in their God-ordained rhythm. As long as they stayed in His pattern, they were in harmony with His purposes, and the earth flourished. Disobedience knocked them out of God's rhythm, however, and the ground became cursed to them. The "rain" ceased. The Lord told Adam,

Because thou…hast eaten of the tree, of which I commanded thee, saying, Thou shalt not eat of it: cursed is the ground for thy sake; in sorrow shalt thou eat of it all the days of thy life; thorns also and thistles shall it bring forth to thee; and thou shalt eat the herb of the field; in the sweat of thy face shalt thou eat bread, till thou return unto the ground; for out of it wast thou taken: for dust thou art, and unto dust shalt thou return. (Genesis 3:17–19)

When God created us in His image, He gave us dominion, authority, and power in the earth. Yet with these privileges comes the responsibility of obedience. The Father has given us the ability to tend all that He has assigned to our hands. Our obedience to His Word establishes a harmony that produces spiritual harvests in our lives in season. When we stay in God's rhythm, seedtime and harvest do not cease. Our ability to harvest is based on our doing what God tells us to do as rulers under His authority.

Jeremiah 8:7 says, *"Yea, the stork in the heaven knoweth her appointed times; and the turtle and the crane and the swallow observe the time of their coming; but my people know not the judgment of the LORD,"* and Psalm 145:15–16 says, *"The eyes of all wait upon thee; and thou givest them their meat in due season. Thou openest thine hand, and satisfiest the desire of every living thing."* The stork, the turtle, the crane, and the swallow know how God works. Human beings seem to be the only ones in God's creation who fight against His purposes. When disobedience wars against the rhythm of God, we can miss the appointed seasons of blessing, healing, and deliverance that have been provided for us.

Seasons of Blessing Are Waiting

It is important to understand that seasons of blessing are waiting for you to enter into them. Again, you can't go through icy storms without knowing that summer is coming. Your life should have regular seasons of fruitfulness because you have been given the ability to *"be fruitful,"* *"multiply,"* *"replenish,"* and *"subdue"* (Genesis 1:28).

> Seasons of blessing are waiting for you to enter into them.

The word *"fruitful"* means to grow or increase. (See *Strong's,* #H6509.) God, through His image in you, intends for you to experience seasons of growth and increase. We have seasons of blessing waiting for us that we can't even imagine. *"Now unto him that is able to do exceeding abundantly above all that we ask or think, according to the power that worketh in us"* (Ephesians 3:20).

Growth involves times of working, sowing, and tending the ground of our concern. It includes waiting, storms, and setbacks, but ultimately there is increase. When our cycle of seasonal increase is broken through disobedience or a lack of understanding of how God works, it can cause our faith to waver. Hopelessness begins to invade our emotions and our wills. In addition, emotional trauma such as child abuse, abandonment, divorce, and other heartbreak can cause our visions of our God-given identity to diminish. The resulting wounds and scars disrupt our cycle of increase.

If you are experiencing a prolonged season of nonproductiveness and continue to struggle with certain issues, it might be due to one of these causes. Seasons are regular, but we can miss them if we don't recognize them or are not ready for them.

> The fruit of a person's life is evidence of his internal condition.

Known By Our Fruits

Just as the fruit of a tree is evidence of its internal condition, the fruit of a person's life is evidence of his internal condition. Jesus said,

> *Ye shall know them by their fruits. Do men gather grapes of thorns, or figs of thistles? Even so every good tree bringeth forth good fruit; but a corrupt tree bringeth forth evil fruit. A good tree cannot bring forth evil fruit, neither can a corrupt tree bring forth good fruit. Every tree that bringeth not forth good fruit is hewn down, and cast into the fire. Wherefore by their fruits ye shall know them.* (Matthew 7:16–20)

If what is in our hearts is good, we will bring forth good fruit. If it is bad, it will bring forth evil fruit. Corruption within

237

is revealed by corrupt behavior. Our words or actions indicate the strengths and weaknesses of our character and emotions. Present behaviors are linked to the past. This is why emotional wounds often produce visible evidence of the trauma in our lives. Old hurts have a bothersome tendency to show up in our present actions.

While emotional hurts can be grievous, they are not an excuse for inappropriate words or behavior. The Bible says that we are accountable for the words we speak, and that we are justified or condemned by our words because they are the outflow of our hearts. (See Matthew 12:36–37.)

A Transformed Nature

If our words and actions reveal an inner problem, what do we do? We go to Jesus and ask Him to change us. The power of the Gospel of Christ will transform our very nature, healing the wounds and removing the scars of the past. Once the Lord heals our wounds, the fruit of our emotions will be changed from negative to positive. As our character is transformed, our fruit takes on a new quality and identity. *"But the fruit of the Spirit is love, joy, peace, longsuffering, kindness, goodness, faithfulness, gentleness, self-control"* (Galatians 5:22–23 NKJV). The outflow of our hearts will reveal that our emotional lives have been delivered. We will become known for something other than the pain and trauma of our pasts. Our cycle of fruitfulness will be restored as God resurrects our faith, hope, and wills, so that we may experience all that He has planned for our lives.

Obedience Is the Key to Breakthrough

Since transformation is usually a process, it may sometimes seem as if God is taking His time in delivering you. If

He is making you wait, then you—or something related to your situation—is not ready. You have to learn to wait for His time because He's changing you while you're waiting. One of the ways God shows us His love is by not giving us more than we can handle. When you are a good steward of what He has already done in your life and trusted to your hands, then He will know that He can entrust you with the rest.

Obedience is the key to our breakthrough as we are waiting. The nation of Israel experienced a delay of the promise due to their disobedience. God had promised to take care of them, and He had proven to them during their captivity that He was a faithful God. He used their bondage, which the enemy had designed to destroy them, to strengthen them for the journey. The Bible says that the more Pharaoh afflicted them, the more they grew and multiplied. (See Exodus 1:12.) God also allowed them to accumulate great riches as they were leaving Egypt. They went into the wilderness with the wealth of their oppressors. (See Exodus 12:35–36.)

> You have to learn to wait for His time because He's changing you while you're waiting.

So God had prepared them for their trip through the wilderness and the difficulty they would face when they reached the land of promise. He also used Moses, the instrument of their deliverance, to teach them His will. He knew that understanding and obeying His ways would enable the people to live victorious lives. Yet the Israelites still missed their season.

Scholars speculate that the entire journey in the wilderness should have taken only a very short period of time. Their breakthrough was just over the horizon. The wilderness was a test orchestrated by God to prove their integrity and appreciation for the deliverance that He had given them. He gave them the promise of the new land to hold on to as they made their way through the desert. God's promises are designed to show His children their privileges in Him and to prompt them to love and serve Him.

Yet the journey that should have taken the Israelites a short time ended up taking them forty years. At another time in Israel's history, God commented on His people's lack of faith. He said they didn't draw the conclusions that should have been obvious to them from the physical world that He had created. *"Neither say they in their heart, Let us now fear the LORD our God, that giveth rain, both the former and the latter, in his season: he reserveth unto us the appointed weeks of the harvest"* (Jeremiah 5:24). Here again, God points to natural seasons as an indicator of what we can expect from Him. Just as He provides seasons on the earth, He will provide for our spiritual, emotional, and physical needs as we look to Him. We can trust Him to do this for us just as we trust the seasons to follow in regular order.

Unfortunately, the Israelites chose not to believe this. When they began to lack food and water, they murmured against Moses and reminisced about the "good old days" in captivity when they supposedly had plenty of meat and bread. (See Exodus 16:2–3.) We should be cautioned by the fact that just because the Promised Land wasn't immediately manifested, they wavered in their faith and ultimately caused the promise to be delayed.

We were not meant to remain in a winter season all the time. Perhaps you see other people being blessed and wonder why God is doing it for them and not for you. Check to see if you are in the rhythm of God's will for your life. Maybe you missed a beat somewhere. This may not be the case, but it's an important issue to look at when seeking healing and deliverance. Jesus said, *"My Father is always at his work to this very day, and I, too, am working"* (John 5:17 NIV). God is continually working to fulfill His purposes. We need to make sure that we are in the right condition to participate in them. *"And let us not be weary in well doing: for in due season we shall reap, if we faint not"* (Galatians 6:9).

We also have to remember the principle that *"faith without works is dead"* (James 2:20, 26). We can have faith for our seasons of harvest, but if we're not walking in obedience, our faith in them is dead, and they will not come to us. If you receive God's commands intellectually or emotionally, but they don't change your will, the Word is not being sown in your life because the ground of your heart is too hard. If we want to start living above our circumstances, we have to do what God has told us to do. He will wait for us to do this. When we do, we'll break into the vision that He has for our lives. There is an appointed time, a new season, when we're going to reap if we keep our heads up and continue walking according to His will.

What should you do if you have made a mistake or disobeyed and fallen away from God? Turn around, just as you would if you missed an exit on the turnpike. Go to the next exit, pay the toll if you have to, and then get back on the right road.

Letting Go of the Past

It is God's will that we move forward in our lives in fulfillment of His purposes. One of the great deterrents of emotional healing is being anchored to past pain, injustice, and struggles. The enemy's strategy is to lock us in our negative pasts. It is the only true weapon he can use to block our progress. If he can cause us to concentrate on where we have been instead of where we are going, he can interrupt God's will for us.

An inability to leave the past behind was one of the major problems of the Israelites. The Lord delivered them from the bondage of Egypt and supplied them with great wealth. Yet when Moses was delayed in his conference with God on the mountain, they took the wealth that He had given them and built a false god to worship. As I wrote earlier, even though they had been delivered from Egypt, Egypt was still in their hearts.

Is your negative past still fixed in your heart? When we operate our lives in true love and submission to God, we can act in obedience when circumstances tempt us to try things our own way. The Bible says, *In all thy ways acknowledge* [God], *and he shall direct thy paths"* (Proverbs 3:6). It is important to understand that getting to the Promised Land was not without its challenges, but God designed the wilderness to build strength, integrity, and love in His people. The Lord had to delay the nation of Israel's breakthrough until the first generation of Israelites had died in the wilderness and all the negative qualities of Egypt—the scars of captivity—had been removed from His people's hearts.

> God designed the wilderness to build strength, integrity, and love in His people.

When Lot and his family were fleeing from Sodom, the Lord instructed them to separate completely from their negative past. As they were leaving the city, however, Lot's wife looked back, and she was turned into a pillar of salt. Unable to separate herself from her former life, she became permanently frozen, her eyes forever locked on her past. Her forward progress was completely stopped, and she was left behind. (See Genesis 19:17, 24–26.)

When Saul disobeyed God and the kingship was taken away from him, the prophet Samuel grieved, but the Lord asked him, *"How long wilt thou mourn for Saul, seeing I have rejected him from reigning over Israel?"* (1 Samuel 16:1). In other words, He was saying, "How long do you intend to mourn over something that you have no power to change?" What an awesome question. God had already chosen another leader for the throne. Samuel was wasting his time being depressed over an unalterable situation.

A wise person once said, "You can't unscramble scrambled eggs." You must simply discard them and start all over again. There are painful things in your past that are very real. They are undeniable, but they are also discardable. The past cannot be changed, but the future can be altered.

> The past cannot be changed, but the future can.

Letting Go of the "Why" Question

One way of releasing the past is by letting go of the "why" question. When you have faced a particularly difficult and injurious situation in the past that leaves you negatively impacted, sometimes the hardest thing to give up is asking, "Why did this happen?" It's all right to ask this question when we are first overtaken by sorrow and grief from a negative circumstance. Remember that, as Jesus endured the cross, He cried out, *"My God, my God, why hast thou forsaken me?"* (Matthew 27:46).

It is not asking why, but continuously questioning God's purposes, that becomes a problem in our deliverance. While seeking to understand our lives is good, it often fails to satisfy or provide relief from our emotional pain. More often than we would like to admit, we won't be able to make sense of the reasons why our mistakes and wounding happened. Looking for answers to unanswerable situations can birth unending frustration. People have spent lifetimes in miserable emotional traps trying to do this. We can't continually agonize over the past. Paul addressed this emotional dilemma when he wrote, *"This one thing I do, forgetting those things which are behind, and reaching forth unto those things which are before, I press toward the mark for the prize of the high calling of God in Christ Jesus"* (Philippians 3:13–14).

Choosing to Let Go of the Past

The biblical principle of forgetting the past is not the same thing as losing the memory of something. The key to understanding this principle is found in the Old Testament where Jeremiah tells us that God does not remember our sin. *"For I will forgive their iniquity, and I will remember their sin no more"* (Jeremiah 31:34).

God is all knowing. This quality is what theologians call *omniscience.* If He knows everything, He cannot experience a memory loss. Instead, He *chooses* not to remember our sins any longer. He does not bring them up with us. He makes a choice to leave them in the sea of forgetfulness.

The path to deliverance from the negative elements of the past is in our God-given ability to choose. We can decide not to rehearse things that were hurtful in the past. We have a tendency to continually go over wounding situations for no other reason than to discuss them again. Often, we look for someone to help us feel better about a situation that is impossible to feel better about. The cyclical rehashing of unresolved situations hinders the healing process.

Letting go of the past is not a method of spiritual denial. We aren't delivered by avoiding unpleasant subjects. The issues and wounds must be healed. They cannot be ignored, or the scars of hurt and destructive behavior will not fade. Confronting the issues in our lives is biblical. (See, for example, Matthew 18:15–17.) We must meet them head on. If we cannot resolve them on our own, we should seek help. The essence of the principle is that we must keep trying to resolve the problem until we do. The Bible speaks of mortifying or rendering ineffective things in our lives that do not honor God. (See Romans 8:13; Colossians 3:5.)

> Deliverance means confronting our wounds and scars and overcoming them.

Deliverance, therefore, has nothing to do with denial. It has everything to do with confronting our wounds and scars and overcoming them. We can establish, as much as possible, the why of our situations. We should also take responsibility for our personal participation in them, asking for forgiveness and forgiving others. Then we should accept God's grace to enable us to deal with any recurring problems, while living each day choosing not to bring up issues that already have been resolved and forgiven.

We have to make an effort to get beyond the things that we need to put behind us. In other words, we should fight the hindrances of our negative past. The wind of resistance requires a determination to progress. We must make up our minds that our wounds will not become monuments to past defeats but rather invitations to victory.

Perseverance and Faith Yield the Fruit of Deliverance

The Bible gives us an excellent example of someone whose season of trial matured into a season of deliverance and blessing.

And, behold, there came a man named Jairus, and he was a ruler of the synagogue: and he fell down at Jesus' feet, and besought him that he would come into his house: for he had one only daughter, about twelve years of age, and she lay a dying. But as he went the people thronged him.

(Luke 8:41–42)

Jairus has come to receive a blessing from the Lord. He is desperate because his daughter is gravely ill. When he approaches Jesus, he falls down before Him in worship and asks Him to heal his daughter. Yet as they make progress in the direction of Jairus's house, Jesus stops to address the problem of another person—the woman with the issue of blood whom we talked about in the previous chapter. (See verses 43–48.)

Jairus has to wait while the Lord addresses another person's illness. He listens as words of comfort and peace are spoken into someone else's life, while his own situation grows more hopeless. To Jairus, it must have seemed as if the Lord was distracted or hadn't prioritized his request as the more important one.

The move of God in your life will test both your faith and your patience. Many of us don't have any problem praying about something, but we have a major problem waiting for God to move on our behalf. Jairus's faith is tested even *after* Jesus is on His way to heal his daughter. There is a delay while someone else is healed. What is happening? Through seeing someone else's miracle, Jairus can strengthen his faith in what God is able to do while he waits for his own miracle. We can do the same.

> *While he yet spake, there cometh one from the ruler of the synagogue's house, saying to him, Thy daughter is dead; trouble not the Master. But when Jesus heard it, he answered him, saying, Fear not: believe only, and she shall be made whole.* (vv. 49–50)

Someone comes from Jairus's home telling him not to bother Jesus any longer because his daughter has died. Yet Jesus doesn't appear to exhibit any alarm about the matter. He simply tells Jairus not to let fear overtake him.

Jairus came to Jesus because he had heard the testimony of others about Him and believed that the Lord could meet his need. He worshipped Jesus, made his request, and received the desired answer. Then the crowd got in his way. The woman who interrupted Jesus' progress toward Jairus's house became a momentary obstacle for him. Perhaps he became discouraged, but he stayed close to Jesus. When the news of his daughter's death came, fear, which is faith's greatest opponent, reveals itself.

> Many of us don't have a problem praying for something, but we do have a problem waiting for God to answer.

Jesus immediately handles his fear by saying, *"Fear not: believe only, and she shall be made whole."* It was as if He was saying, "Don't you dare start being afraid now. Keep trusting and believe, and you will receive the answer to your need."

And when he came into the house, he suffered no man to go in, save Peter, and James, and John, and the father and the mother of the maiden. And all wept, and bewailed her: but he said, Weep not; she is not dead, but sleepeth. And they laughed him to scorn, knowing that she was dead. And he put them all out. (vv. 51–54)

When Jesus arrives at Jairus's house, He takes Peter, James, John, and the parents of the child and goes inside. There are plenty of people around—many of them probably paid mourners—who are wailing and crying because they believe the problem is beyond a solution. Jesus tells them to stop weeping. He sees the problem from a position of power, while they see it from a position of weakness. Their faith is nonexistent, and they laugh at Him. The Bible says that *"they laughed him to scorn, knowing that she was dead"* (v. 53). They mocked Jesus because, in their eyes, He was being ridiculous. Their perception of the situation was limited by their inability to change it, so Jesus put them out of the house.

Jesus made them leave because healing and miracles can be hindered by unbelief. If Jesus could be hindered in this way, we certainly can. We have to guard against unbelief as we seek deliverance. There are things in our lives that appear to be dead, but Jesus sees them as alive. The only reason they haven't yet manifested their resurrection is that we haven't believed they can live again. Remember that when you have lost hope and feel dead on the inside because of the hurts that you bear, there is help for you in Jesus.

[Jesus] *took her by the hand, and called, saying, Maid, arise. And her spirit came again, and she arose straightway: and he commanded to give her meat. And her parents were astonished: but he charged them that they should tell no man what was done.* (vv. 54–56)

Jairus waited as another stepped in line before him and received the miracle he had asked for. He watched his faith have no apparent immediate effect on his problem. Time became the opponent of his faith, fear attacked his patience, and death seemed to seal shut the problem forever. Once again, we encounter an individual whose problem grows more severe after he draws closer to Jesus. But Jairus goes the extra mile, letting nothing get in the way of his daughter's healing, and she is restored to him.

In the Fullness of Time

Why do you think Jesus didn't just say a word to correct the situation at Jairus's house? He decided to heal the girl in person rather than speaking the miracle into existence, as He had done for others. (See, for example, Matthew 8:5–13.) I think that Jesus allowed the delay in which the daughter died in order to show Jairus the extent of His power in being able to raise the dead. The Lord already knew that the child would recover regardless of what it looked like to others, so He wasn't in a rush.

Jesus' affirmation that He would heal the daughter was the announcement of a new season of life for her and the end of a season of stress for Jairus. Most people believe that the season begins when the blessing begins, yet the season begins when we first receive a word from God that addresses our circumstances. We are to be *"fully persuaded that, what he had promised, he was able also to perform"* (Romans 4:21).

Abraham received a revelation that announced the end of Sarah's season of barrenness and his season of lacking an heir. Yet they had to endure several more challenges before the answer to their prayer was born. Joseph's promotion was announced in a dream, but he ended up in a pit, enslaved, and imprisoned. All this happened after he received a yes from God. He had to wait in faith for the physical manifestation of his dream. David was anointed by Samuel to be king when he was still tending sheep. Yet not only was he sent right back to the sheep, but he also encountered all types of difficulties for more than a decade, which must have made him long for the relative comfort, security, and peace of shepherding. It took years before the full promise of his kingship was fulfilled.

Your faith and patience may endure a hard test as you seek healing from your wounds and scars. If this happens, remember that none of the above situations negated the fact that each of these individual's seasons had arrived. The same is true for your situation. No matter how difficult it looks now, your season of fulfillment and deliverance is a reality because God has promised it.

The Lord wants to resurrect your hope and future.

As Jesus raised Jairus's daughter, the Lord wants to resurrect your hope and future. Perhaps you experienced a trauma early in life that has hindered your emotional development and caused you to lose opportunity and possibility. He wants to heal the internal issue that has plagued you for so many years. He is calling you to live again. Jesus will restore your life so that you may go on to mature in Him and live in His purposes.

A Passion for Victory

Expectation resurrects hope and faith, which lead to deliverance. Instead of thinking of your wounds as a sign of your destruction, consider them an indicator of the victory God has promised you. Experienced soldiers become more determined when the enemy wounds them. It inspires them to fight harder to survive. When our enemy wounds us, he is attempting to take something that God has given us, and we must fight back.

In John 10:10, Jesus said, *"The thief does not come except to steal, and to kill, and to destroy. I have come that they may have life, and that they may have it more abundantly"* (NKJV). The enemy comes to destroy, but God has given you the offer of abundant life. Wounds and scars are the weapons the enemy would love to use to steal your dreams, kill your hope, and destroy your faith, so your perception of them must change. Again, your wounds and scars are not a signal of defeat. They are your invitation to victory.

The victory is not just for you. Those close to you—your spouse, children, parents, and friends—will benefit from your deliverance. There is an opportunity, a relationship, or a loved one waiting for you to press past your scars. You have waited long enough. You can't change the past but you can address it, let it go, and move on. Your disappointment, faith in God, and expectation have been working together to produce a passion for victory.

Get Ready to Reap

Now is your time of deliverance. If you have fallen, get up again. If you have been defeated, try again. If you have been rejected, make a decision to love again. Hold on to the promise of God. His Word is the substance of your expectation, and it cannot fail. You are on the threshold of being healed and delivered.

When you have the promise of God, even though you're going through a wilderness, you can see what God intends to do for you at the appointed time of your breakthrough. Seed has been sown, and it is growing within you, preparing for a harvest. Get ready to reap! *They that sow in tears shall reap in joy. He that goeth forth and weepeth, bearing precious seed, shall doubtless come again with rejoicing, bringing his sheaves with him"* (Psalm 126:5–6).

Chapter Thirteen

Healed Without Scars

I remember it, but it doesn't hurt anymore.

He was a man who believed in doing the right thing, avoided offending others, and took care of his responsibilities. His great wealth and success were the product of faith, hard work, and God's favor. Raising his family in the best way he could, he equipped his children with the right foundations: Lessons of responsibility, family, loyalty, and faith were taught at every possible opportunity. Home was a peaceful place filled with a sense of security. It was also a festive place with regular gatherings where friends and relatives were always welcome.

The man's sons and daughters were given a foundation for success. All they had to do was follow the example of their father. He'd always been a pillar of strength and consistency. They knew that their father was a great man—a man to be admired and imitated.

Like all good fathers, the man worried that the lessons he taught his children might fall on deaf ears, but he hoped that the seeds of wisdom would take root and one day produce fruits of maturity. He was concerned that the destiny of his children be positive and not tragic, so he did everything in his power to assure that this was the case. What he discovered, however, was that human ability has its limitations. Sometimes, events beyond our control threaten to shatter our lives.

Experiencing one of the most gut-wrenching ordeals of all time, Job watches as everything he's worked so hard to build disintegrates in less than a day. He undergoes an intense fire of suffering. Unknown to him, this ordeal is part of God's plan for perfecting his life. He comes to a deeper understanding of his Creator's power and faithfulness, and He brings glory to God through his steadfast trustworthiness and praise. Contrary to popular belief, it is not victory that shapes us, but adversity. Tribulation molds and defines the character of our lives. Let's look more closely at the life of Job, which is recorded in the book that bears his name.

It is not victory that shapes us, but adversity.

The Worst Day of His Life

The day began as any other day. Apparently, the evening before, all had been peaceful, without any indication of what was to come. I imagine Job surveying all that he owned. His investments are intact. His family's security remains unchallenged, and those who are helping him to build his success seem eager to continue their support.

Then, unexpectedly, a messenger brings bad news. Neighboring peoples have attacked Job's herd of oxen and donkeys and carried them off after killing those who were taking care of them. In the past, Job has always addressed any problems immediately and brought things back into order with confidence and experience. Since a hostile takeover is not uncommon in his environment, maybe he says to himself, "I have worked through tougher times than this. I will rebuild my strength, and everything will be all right."

Yet, as he is regaining his perspective, he receives another message. A natural disaster has destroyed another part of his herds, and more of his workers have been killed. Perhaps this time he thinks, "I can't complain. These things happen, but...what is going on?" An element of confusion creeps in. Unbelievably, more bad news arrives. Another raiding party has carried off the rest of his herds, and more of his servants have been slain.

In his growing alarm, maybe he thinks, "At least my family is safe." Then the worst happens. A fierce wind, perhaps a hurricane or tornado, strikes with sudden fury, and all his children are killed while they are attending a party in the oldest son's home.

Job's life has been permanently altered. He mourns deeply, yet holds on to his faith, saying, *"The LORD gave, and the LORD hath taken away; blessed be the name of the LORD"* (Job 1:21). Looking at his entire life, he acknowledges that life is a series of seasons, some good and some bad, and that we must expect to experience both. At one point, he says to his wife, *"Shall we indeed accept good from God, and shall we not accept adversity?"* (Job 2:10 NKJV).

Abandoned by Everyone

Then Job's health fails. People close to him begin to challenge all that he believes and has based his life upon: His wife abandons him emotionally at the time of his greatest need, and his friends contribute only criticism. Maybe they look at his situation as an opportunity to verbalize hidden feelings of jealousy, hoping that he is less than he appears to be. Adversity will force your friends and your enemies to reveal themselves.

Job tries to declare his innocence to his friends, but to no avail. They believe he is getting what he deserves for some secret infraction. Job continues to love God, but he wants answers about why he is going through all these troubles.

Job's Healing and Restoration

Finally, mercifully, God speaks. Though He has allowed Job to go through this test, He demonstrates that He has always been in control of the circumstances and that Job has never been out of His protective care. Job prays for the friends who criticized him, and the Lord reverses his situation, causing him to be more materially blessed than he was before the crisis.

> God is always in control of the circumstances, and we are never out of His protective care.

Sometimes, difficult situations happen to good people through no fault of their own. Life can seem extremely unfair. Yet in everything Job went through, he held on to his faith and his character, and his life became defined by his experience. While he had been deeply wounded, he emerged from his experience healed without scars. God mended the hurts and filled the voids in his life. He gave Job twice as much wealth as he had before his ordeal. Of course, nothing can replace the lives of his children. Yet God gives him seven more sons and three more daughters. They bring joy to Job and seem to play a part in his restoration as their presence and love heals the hurt in his heart. Job can walk in confidence and strength once again, understanding more deeply the power and faithfulness of God, and being strengthened in his own faith and character.

Was God Caught Off Guard?

Life has a tendency to carry us into situations where we never would have gone voluntarily. Job's story teaches us much about the tests and trials that we undergo. Job wanted to understand the reason for his suffering while he was going through it. At times, I'm so shocked by some things that happen to me that I subconsciously think God has been caught off guard by them, too. If He had known about my troubles, wouldn't He have prevented them? Often, I'll find myself questioning God, as Job eventually began to.

> The faithfulness and love of the Father is with us at all times.

We think we would handle things better if God would just give us a preview of what we were going to face. We imagine that if He gave us a glimpse of what was going to happen, we could have a sense of confidence that He was in control. This is probably not the case, however. Even if we knew what troubles we would face, we would likely still ask God *why* we had to go through them.

What we can be assured of is that the faithfulness and love of the Father is with us at all times. He is working out His plans behind the scenes of our lives. Gaining personal transformation and a deeper relationship with God through our trials is a process that takes time. We often don't recognize at first how God is working our troubles for good in our lives. Yet as we entrust ourselves to His care, He will see us through.

The Greater Grace of Preservation

Does it ever seem to you that, the hotter the situation you're in, the more time God seems to take in doing something about it? That appears to have been the case with Job, but his story reveals a powerful truth into how the Father heals us without scars when we suffer the wounds of life. The story of his survival through all his troubles reveals what I believe is one of the greater graces of God.

In the midst of adversity, we are looking for deliverance. The greater grace is not deliverance, however, but *preservation*. Why? God's resurrection power is revealed when we are sustained in a difficulty that causes others to give up. The forces of the world and the enemy are going to come against us, and we must learn to keep loving, trusting, and worshipping God in difficult times in order to persevere in fulfilling His purposes for our lives and for the world.

> The greater grace is not deliverance, but *preservation*.

Most people just want to talk about being blessed. They don't want to mention that, in order to be blessed, we're going to have undergo persecution. I've found that before the blessing comes, persecution comes to discourage me about what God is about to do in my life. The enemy tries to preempt us from receiving the blessing. Persecution will cause us to miss God if we concentrate more on what the enemy is doing rather than what God is going to do.

When you decide to believe in the love and promises of God, the devil is not going to leave you alone. The moment you begin to move in God's will for your life, persecution may break out as it never has before. As happened to Job, people whom you thought you could depend on may misunderstand and turn on you.

The enemy knows that God wants to preserve you in the fire, so he causes the fire to be more intense so you'll give up in the midst of it. When Shadrach, Meshach, and Abednego were thrown into the fiery furnace, it had been heated up seven times hotter than usual. When the fire is that hot, only faith will make you walk into it to encounter the preserving presence of God.

God wants to deliver you *in* the fire before He moves you out of it. The difficulty may be that you have not yet learned to walk freely with Him in the fire. You must learn to be in the presence of God in the midst of adversity. When you do, you'll be amazed, saying, "That's strange. I can breathe in here. My clothes are not burned. I'm not even perspiring. I should be consumed, but I'm walking around in the very thing that should be destroying me."

> God wants to deliver you in the fire before He moves you out of it.

Noah was preserved in a boat in the midst of a flood that killed everybody except those who were under the protection of God. Moses and the Israelites were preserved by walking through the very thing that should have drowned them. Instead, God transformed the Red Sea into a way of deliverance for them. When Jesus experienced death and lay in the tomb, the very thing that should have held Him forever was just a holding area until it was time for Him to come walking out in resurrection power.

Thriving in What Should Have Consumed Us

Have you been through some things that should have marked you for life, but instead served to strengthen and free you? Perhaps you were depressed for a long time, but after drawing close to God in search of healing, you woke up one morning and said, "I don't feel the heaviness any longer." If you haven't yet had this experience, God wants to loose you in the midst of the fire so that it *can* be your testimony.

We need to stop looking for a way out of tight situations. The path to deliverance is in being able to function in what should consume us. Shadrach, Meshach, and Abednego did not lose their praise even though they were thrown into the fire. God says, in effect, "The enemy can turn up the fire as hot as hell, but you will not die in it because you belong to Me. They haven't made a fire hot enough to consume your life. There isn't a situation tight enough to hold you down."

> It looks as if you are being consumed, but you are being consecrated for God's purposes.

Evidently, it was so hot outside the furnace that the strong men who threw Shadrach, Meshach, and Abednego into the fire were killed. There are some things that have destroyed other people, but when you walk through the same thing, you are preserved by almighty God because you have remained in His presence and have received His sustaining power. To other people, it looks as if you are being consumed, but you are actually being consecrated for His purposes.

No Signs of the Fire

The Bible says that not a hair on the heads of the young Hebrew men was singed, and their clothes didn't even smell like fire. The situation left them with no long-lasting effects. After you are preserved in your trial, other people will be amazed at the quality of your life. They'll seek some sign of what you went through, but they won't be able to find it. They'll look for singed hair and the smell of smoke—some small evidence that you were defeated by the same thing that they were. They'll look for it in your attitude, and they'll look for it in your words, but they'll be discouraged because they won't be able to find it. Then they'll say, "After what you went through, you ought to be depressed or an alcoholic. How did you survive?" You'll answer, "I don't know. All I know is that my God is able. I didn't know it before I went into the fire, but now I know by experience that my God is able to save." After his ordeal, Job acknowledged to God, *My ears had heard of you but now my eyes have seen you* (Job 42:5 NIV).

> After God preserves you, the memories of the fire will not hurt as they used to.

You may tell others that you were abused or given away as a child, and they will say, "What? I would never have thought that about you." Or they'll exclaim, "What do you mean you're a pastor? Weren't you one of the biggest drug dealers in the state?" If you're at a family gathering, and someone brings up a situation from the past just to see how you'll react, it's all right because they can't hurt you any longer. Your past no longer stops you from moving forward.

After God preserves you in the fire, the memories of that fire might still bring you some discomfort, but they won't hurt as they used to. You may shed a tear over some things when you think about them, but you won't break down as you formerly did because God has preserved and delivered you.

You'll remember the situation, but it won't hurt anymore. Perhaps you came from a broken home, but now you've established your own home, and the hurt has been transformed into wholeness. Perhaps you were abused, but now you are healed, and your testimony is that the Lord is good and worthy to be praised. You've been through the fire. You've been through the flood. But it does not hurt anymore because God has healed you without scars.

When we *try* not to remember our past, that is when we run into difficulty. But when we confess our mistakes and sins to God, and when we give over to Him the pain and abuse we've received from others, we become free and can say, "It happened, but now I'm delivered. I remember the flames. I remember the heat. I remember what bound me, but it doesn't hurt anymore."

We don't want to forget the fire completely because our coming through it becomes our encouragement in our next test. We know that if the first fire didn't consume us, then what we're facing now can also be overcome.

Allow Jesus to Heal You

Are you in the fire right now? God wants to preserve you and heal you without scars. Jesus says in Revelation 3:20, *"Behold, I stand at the door and knock. If anyone hears My voice and opens the door, I will come in to him and dine with him, and he with Me"* (NKJV). God wants to walk through the door of your negative experience, damaged emotions, and lost expectation. He desires an invitation into the emotional refuge you have created that protects you from further hurt but shields you from full healing. Let Him into that dark place. His desire is to set you free. He has the power to heal you of all the issues in your life. When you let Him in, your hope and expectation will be reborn as the light of renewed purpose and restoration pushes away the darkness of the past.

Jesus will do for you what you are unable to do for yourself. God sent Jesus to heal your mind, will, and emotions, which have been fragmented by your negative experiences. He will free you from the captivity of the past that holds you back from a full life.

Jesus brings beauty in exchange for the ugliness of the past. As hurtful and hopeless as your feelings may be, you have God's promise of restoration. The Lord will exchange the sadness, mourning, and pain of lost hope for the joy of His presence. He wants to remove the image of defeat and heaviness from your life and renew your dreams and aspirations. Your damaged life can be rebuilt by His power. Life with God removes you from the nonproductive isolation and alienation that trauma produces. You will have new, positive relationships as He aligns your life with His purposes.

> God will give you a new identity with a new level of expectation.

God will give you a new identity with a new level of expectation. This identity will be based on the foundation of peace that comes from a relationship with Him. His original intent for you will be restored. This intent is a life of productivity, power, and victory. He wants to stabilize the emotional roller coaster of your depression, anger, fear, and hopelessness, and reconnect you with purpose and joy. He wants to give you the ability to persevere in and recover from all the challenges of life.

Jesus is not looking at what you have become, but at what you will be. He has a vision of you in His mind that you can still fulfill. That person is healed without scars. God wants to use the apparent negatives of your past as the components for a future of wholeness and strength.

The realm of impossibility is the place of opportunity with God. In that place, you will be healed without scars.

About the Author

Bishop David G. Evans is the pastor of Bethany Baptist Church in Lindenwold, New Jersey, and prelate of the Abundant Harvest Fellowship of Churches. An anointed and gifted teacher, preacher, and administrator, Bishop Evans is known for his down-to-earth, life-applicable, realistic approach to preaching and teaching God's holy Word.

A dean's list student and multisport athlete, Bishop Evans graduated from Lincoln University in 1973, where he majored in economics and education. He has served as a vice president for a commercial lending corporation and as the owner and operator of a commercial cleaning company.

Bishop Evans accepted Christ in September 1976 and was called into the fivefold ministry in 1979. He was licensed to preach and then ordained by the Bethany Baptist Association in 1989. This Spirit-led visionary loves the people of God and delights in shepherding his multicultural flock. Called to this profound responsibility in 1990, Bishop Evans' sensitivity and obedience to God's direction has caused Bethany Baptist Church to experience tremendous growth. Numerous people have been saved and multilevel, Bible-based ministries have been implemented to meet every possible need. Membership has grown from seventy-five to eighteen thousand.

Bishop Evans was called to the office of bishop in March 1996 as Presiding Officer of the Abundant Harvest Fellowship of Churches—a full-gospel fellowship with a fundamental mission to evangelize the lost, edify the believer, equip the saints for ministry, and grow the local church.

Recognizing the magnitude of needs throughout the southern New Jersey region, the vision has extended to the creation of a nonprofit community development corporation, Generations, Inc. Under Bishop Evans' leadership as chairman of the board of directors, Generations, Inc., addresses the life-span needs of southern New Jersey residents through economic development and a broad range of human services.

**Free at Last:
Removing the Past from Your Future
(with Study Guide and CD)**
Larry Huch

You can break free from your past! Don't let what has happened to you and your family hold you back in life. You can find freedom from depression, anger, abuse, insecurity, and addiction in Jesus Christ. Pastor Larry Huch reveals powerful truths from Scripture that enabled him and many others to quickly break the destructive chains in their lives and receive God's blessings. Learn the secret to true freedom and you, too, can regain your joy and hope, experience divine health, mend broken relationships, walk in true prosperity—body, soul, and spirit.

ISBN: 0-88368-428-4 • Trade with CD • 272 pages

** W**
WHITAKER
HOUSE

proclaiming the power of the Gospel through the written word
visit our website at www.whitakerhouse.com

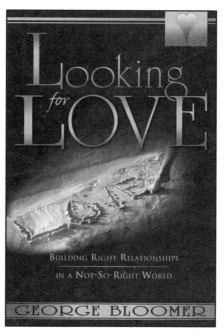

Looking for Love:
Building Right Relationships in a Not-So-Right World
(with CD)

George G. Bloomer

Deep down, each of us wants to experience a relationship that will give us the love, support, and intimate friendship we so desperately desire. If you're ready to discover the essential keys to experiencing lasting love, then let George Bloomer show you the way to establishing godly relationships that will stand the test of time. Whether you're married or still looking for that special someone, find out how to develop deeper intimacy by growing closer to God. Then start enjoying loving, lasting relationships far beyond all you could ever ask or imagine!

ISBN: 0-88368-991-X • Trade with CD • 176 pages

ш

WHITAKER
HOUSE

proclaiming the power of the Gospel through the written word
visit our website at www.whitakerhouse.com

The Principles and Power of Vision
Dr. Myles Munroe

Whether you are a businessperson, a homemaker, a student, or a head of state, best-selling author Dr. Myles Munroe explains how you can make your dreams and hopes a living reality. Your success is not dependent on the state of the economy or what the job market is like. You do not need to be hindered by the limited perceptions of others or by a lack of resources. Discover time-tested principles that will enable you to fulfill your vision no matter who you are or where you come from. You were not meant for a mundane or mediocre life. Revive your passion for living, pursue your dream, discover your vision—and find your true life.

ISBN: 0-88368-951-0 • Hardcover • 240 pages

ƱƱ
WHITAKER
HOUSE

proclaiming the power of the Gospel through the written word
visit our website at www.whitakerhouse.com

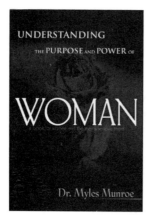

Women of every culture and society are facing the dilemma of identity. To live successfully in today's world, women need a new awareness of who they are and new skills to meet life's challenges. Best-selling author Dr. Myles Munroe helps women to discover their God-given purpose and potential. Whether you are a woman or a man, married or single, this book will help you to understand *the woman as she was meant to be.*

Understanding the Purpose and Power of Woman
Dr. Myles Munroe
ISBN: 0-88368-671-6 • Trade • 208 pages

Understanding the Purpose and Power of Men
Dr. Myles Munroe
ISBN: 0-88368-725-9 • Trade • 224 pages

The male is in crisis. Today, the world is sending out conflicting signals about what it means to be a man. Many men are questioning who they are and what roles they fulfill in life—as males, as husbands, and as fathers. Best-selling author Dr. Myles Munroe examines cultural attitudes toward men and discusses the purpose God has given them. Discover the destiny and potential of *the man as he was meant to be.*

WHITAKER
HOUSE

proclaiming the power of the Gospel through the written word
visit our website at www.whitakerhouse.com

You hunger to live in the presence of God. You yearn to know the Father's heart in an intimate way. You desire revelation and passionate encounters with the Almighty. You want to spend time away from the world, getting to know the Father in a deeper way. If you long to experience a greater intimacy with the Father, *The Secret Place* will draw you in and change your life!

The Secret Place: Passionately Pursuing His Presence
Dr. Dale A. Fife
ISBN: 0-88368-715-1 • Trade • 240 pages

The Hidden Kingdom: Journey into the Heart of God
Dr. Dale A. Fife
ISBN: 0-88368-947-2 • Trade • 256 pages

There are divine moments in life when you turn a corner and are astounded by unexpected, breathtaking vistas that you never imagined. Suddenly your world is changed forever. You have entered a supernatural realm, an eternal dimension, where Jesus is Lord and creation itself shouts His glory. The brilliantly illuminating revelation in *The Hidden Kingdom* will catapult you into such an experience. If you want an empowered life, this book will lead you on a journey into the heart of God.

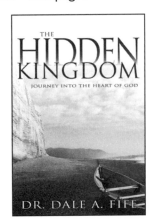

UU
WHITAKER
HOUSE

proclaiming the power of the Gospel through the written word
visit our website at www.whitakerhouse.com

Healed Without Scars Study Companion:
A Personal Healing Journal
David G. Evans
with Danielle Horner

For years, author David G. Evans has helped people from all walks of life discover how to live in victory. His life-changing book, *Healed Without Scars,* is filled with contemporary and biblical accounts of those who have emerged victorious from life's tests and trials. Now, *Healed Without Scars Study Companion: A Personal Healing Journal* enables you to explore deeper insights and thought-provoking questions from the book and to discover powerful healing truths and principles for your own life.

ISBN: 0-88368-661-4 • Workbook • 144 pages

山

WHITAKER
HOUSE

proclaiming the power of the Gospel through the written word
visit our website at www.whitakerhouse.com